Communications in Computer and Information Science 2453

Series Editors

Rationale
The CCIS series is devoted to the publication of proceedings of computer science conferences. Its aim is to efficiently disseminate original research results in informatics in printed and electronic form. While the focus is on publication of peer-reviewed full papers presenting mature work, inclusion of reviewed short papers reporting on work in progress is welcome, too. Besides globally relevant meetings with internationally representative program committees guaranteeing a strict peer-reviewing and paper selection process, conferences run by societies or of high regional or national relevance are also considered for publication.

Topics
The topical scope of CCIS spans the entire spectrum of informatics ranging from foundational topics in the theory of computing to information and communications science and technology and a broad variety of interdisciplinary application fields.

Information for Volume Editors and Authors
Publication in CCIS is free of charge. No royalties are paid, however, we offer registered conference participants temporary free access to the online version of the conference proceedings on SpringerLink (http://link.springer.com) by means of an http referrer from the conference website and/or a number of complimentary printed copies, as specified in the official acceptance email of the event.

CCIS proceedings can be published in time for distribution at conferences or as post-proceedings, and delivered in the form of printed books and/or electronically as USBs and/or e-content licenses for accessing proceedings at SpringerLink. Furthermore, CCIS proceedings are included in the CCIS electronic book series hosted in the SpringerLink digital library at http://link.springer.com/bookseries/7899. Conferences publishing in CCIS are allowed to use Online Conference Service (OCS) for managing the whole proceedings lifecycle (from submission and reviewing to preparing for publication) free of charge.

Publication process
The language of publication is exclusively English. Authors publishing in CCIS have to sign the Springer CCIS copyright transfer form, however, they are free to use their material published in CCIS for substantially changed, more elaborate subsequent publications elsewhere. For the preparation of the camera-ready papers/files, authors have to strictly adhere to the Springer CCIS Authors' Instructions and are strongly encouraged to use the CCIS LaTeX style files or templates.

Abstracting/Indexing
CCIS is abstracted/indexed in DBLP, Google Scholar, EI-Compendex, Mathematical Reviews, SCImago, Scopus. CCIS volumes are also submitted for the inclusion in ISI Proceedings.

How to start
To start the evaluation of your proposal for inclusion in the CCIS series, please send an e-mail to ccis@springer.com.

Salil Kanhere · Raja Jurdak · Joy Parkinson ·
Bhavani Sridharan · Shantanu Pal ·
Kamanashis Biswas
Editors

Distributed Ledger Technology

8th International Symposium, SDLT 2024
Brisbane, QLD, Australia, November 28–29, 2024
Revised Selected Papers

Springer

Editors
Salil Kanhere
University of New South Wales
Sydney, NSW, Australia

Raja Jurdak
Queensland University of Technology
Brisbane, QLD, Australia

Joy Parkinson
Australian Catholic University
Brisbane, QLD, Australia

Bhavani Sridharan
Australian Catholic University
Melbourne, VIC, Australia

Shantanu Pal
Deakin University
Melbourne, VIC, Australia

Kamanashis Biswas
Australian Catholic University
Brisbane, QLD, Australia

ISSN 1865-0929 ISSN 1865-0937 (electronic)
Communications in Computer and Information Science
ISBN 978-981-96-4441-4 ISBN 978-981-96-4442-1 (eBook)
https://doi.org/10.1007/978-981-96-4442-1

This Springer imprint is published by the registered company Springer Nature Singapore Pte Ltd.
The registered company address is: 152 Beach Road, #21-01/04 Gateway East, Singapore 189721, Singapore

Preface

This volume presents the proceedings of the 8th International Symposium on Distributed Ledger Technology (SDLT 2024), held in Brisbane, Queensland, Australia, on November 28–29, 2024. It features 8 full papers and 1 short paper, carefully selected from 31 submissions through a rigorous review process. The contributions in this collection explore current systems and propose innovative solutions, providing a robust scientific foundation for the advancement of Distributed Ledger Technology applications.

November 2024

Salil Kanhere
Raja Jurdak
Joy Parkinson
Bhavani Sridharan
Shantanu Pal
Kamanashis Biswas

Organization

General Chairs

Salil Kanhere	The University of New South Wales, Australia
Joy Parkinson	Australian Catholic University, Australia
Bhavani Sridharan	Australian Catholic University, Australia

Program Committee Chairs

Biswas, Kamanashis	Australian Catholic University, Australia
Jurdak, Raja	Queensland University of Technology, Australia
Pal, Shantanu	Deakin University, Australia

Program Committee Members

Alam, Zaidul	CSIRO, Australia
Allen, Darcy	RMIT University, Australia
Ashley, Paul	Anonyome Labs, Australia
Biswas, Sujit	City St George's, University of London, UK
Biswas, Kamanashis	Australian Catholic University, Australia
Cao, Shoufeng	The University of Queensland, Australia
Chen, Shiping	CSIRO, Australia
Chowdhury, Mohammad Jabed Morshed	La Trobe University, Australia
Chowdhury, Niaz	EdTech, UK
Donaghy, Katrina	Water Ledger Australia, Australia
Dong, Naipeng	The University of Queensland, Australia
Ferdous, Md Sadek	BRAC University, Bangladesh
Hou, Zhe	Griffith University, Australia
Jeyakumar, Samantha	University of Jaffna, Sri Lanka
Johnson, Sandra	Queensland University of Technology, Australia
Jurdak, Raja	Queensland University of Technology, Australia
Kizhakkethottam, Jubilant J.	Saintgits College of Engineering, India
Muthukumarasamy, Vallipuram	Griffith University, Australia
Paik, Helen	The University of New South Wales, Australia
Pal, Shantanu	Deakin University, Australia

Patil, Vishwas	IIT Bombay, India
Pillai, Babu	Southern Cross University, Australia
Robinson, Peter	Immutable, Australia
Usman, Muhammad	Edge Hill University, UK
Xue, Yinxing	University of Science and Technology of China, China
Zelenyanszki, Dorottya	Griffith University, Australia

Reviewers

Alam, Zaidul	CSIRO, Australia
Allen, Darcy	RMIT University, Australia
Ashley, Paul	Anonyome Labs, Australia
Bai, Guangdong	The University of Queensland, Australia
Biswas, Kamanashis	Australian Catholic University, Australia
Biswas, Sujit	City St George's, University of London, UK
Bukhari, Sadaf	Beijing Institute of Technology, China
Cao, Shoufeng	The University of Queensland, Australia
Chen, Shiping	CSIRO, Australia
Chowdhury, Mohammad Jabed Morshed	La Trobe University, Australia
Donaghy, Katrina	Water Ledger Australia, Australia
Dong, Naipeng	The University of Queensland, Australia
Ferdous, Md Sadek	BRAC University, Bangladesh
Hou, Zhe	Griffith University, Australia
Jeyakumar, Samantha	University of Jaffna, Sri Lanka
Johnson, Sandra	Queensland University of Technology, Australia
Kizhakkethottam, Jubilant J.	Saintgits College of Engineering, India
Pal, Shantanu	Deakin University, Australia
Patil, Vishwas	IIT Bombay, India
Pillai, Babu	Southern Cross University, Australia
Robinson, Peter	Immutable, Australia
Usman, Muhammad	Edge Hill University, UK
Xue, Yinxing	University of Science and Technology of China, China
Zelenyanszki, Dorottya	Griffith University, Australia

Contents

Academic Track

Topographic Attribute Map-Based Visualisation to Uncover Behaviour Patterns in Blockchain Networks

Awarjana Perera[1](✉), Samantha Tharani Jeyakumar[1,2], Liat Rozenberg[1], and Vallipuram Muthukkumarasamy[1]

[1] Griffith University, Brisbane, Australia
awarjana.perera@griffithuni.edu.au
[2] University of Jaffna, Jaffna, Sri Lanka

Abstract. Blockchain and its derived technologies lead the future generation to a trust-based digital world. Being decentralised, immutable, and transparent has offered integrity, availability, authenticity, and non-repudiation for shared assets of the agricultural, medical, education and financial sectors. Pseudo-anonymity is one of the crucial properties of the blockchain network that preserves the privacy of the participants by hiding their original information. However, this feature is being exploited via receiving illegal gains such as ransomware settlements, Ponzi schemes, scams, phishing and dark market trades in the form of crypto assets. These rising crimes have become a challenge for law enforcement authorities, forensic analysts, and financial authorities, necessitating the development of more sophisticated detection methods. Understanding the mechanisms used by criminals requires domain experts' knowledge. Further, as the native structure of the blockchain data is complex and large in volume, this raises a challenge in analysis. This paper proposes a methodology to use Topographic Attribute Maps (TAM), a novel data visualisation method for visualising tactics behind illegal activities based on the layout of the transaction network and the characteristics of the transactions. The results show that the proposed visualisation technique enriches the existing attribute-based graph as digital evidence, via classifying with contour lines and colour maps, positioning the accounts in the network as nodes, and representing the links with other accounts. These features of TAM are comprehensible for professionals from other domains, especially those from non-technical backgrounds.

Keywords: blockchain network · malicious activity · data visualisation · graph modeling · behaviour patterns · topographic attribute map

1 Introduction

Blockchain technology has gained significant attention in the recent past. The first form of electronic cash 'Bitcoin', introduced the concept of blockchain technology in 2008 [11]. Blockchain is a distributed ledger technology that records

S. Kanhere et al. (Eds.): SDLT 2024, CCIS 2453, pp. 3–18, 2025.
https://doi.org/10.1007/978-981-96-4442-1_1

transactions in chronological order. Blocks are the transaction data holders that keep the records immutable using hash pointers. The validation of the transaction data is achieved using consensus mechanisms [12]. These features build blockchain as a trustworthy platform with properties such as availability, integrity and non-reputation. This trustworthy platform creates a need for blockchain technology in various industries for tracking supply chain processes, managing health systems data, and ensuring data reliability in Internet of Things (IoT) networks [9,21].

The ransomware attack targeting medical firm 'Change Healthcare' in early 2024 has been one of the most disruptive in years. One of the affiliates of the hackers (AlphV or BlackCat) behind the attack points out that the cybercriminals received 22 million USD transactions over the Bitcoin network[1]. Pseudonymity in blockchain inherently provides obfuscation, ensuring that related information remains unavailable. This makes tracing the movement of digital assets related to the settlements for cyber-attacks, Ponzi schemes, money laundering, or dark market trades more difficult. The incidents related to the illegal gains over blockchain networks bring the necessity to monitor the transactions and improve the security of the network via monitoring the activities in the blockchain network. The interactive monitoring for blockchain transaction data includes identifying the participants' behavioural changes, providing early warning for the changes in the number of transactions, and the values of the crypto assets transferring within the participants.

The transaction data of the blockchain network is large in volume and complex in structure which causes significant challenges in the development of the monitoring platform. The representations in the tabular or text-based format do not represent the interactions between the participants and the dynamic changes in their behaviour. The information presented in the existing monitoring platforms such as BitcoinInfo [1], Infura [4], and EtherScan [3] needs the guidance of domain experts for making decisions [9]. Addressing these limitations needs a paradigm shift in the elements of visualisation, may provide a colour code for the suspicious behaviour, group participants based on the similarity, and arrange them based on the influence. These visual outcomes encourage the decision-making of end users such as financial regulators, forensic analysts, and legal authorities via digital footprints.

The existing monitoring approaches mainly deal with attributed graphs [5,7,17,19]. The attributed graph-based visualisation provides an experience for the interactions between the participants via connecting them using the information of their corresponding transactions. In the attributed graphs, positioning of the nodes and grouping nodes based on the similarity needs additional mechanisms. Topographic Attribute Maps are a novel visualisation of attributed graphs, combined with techniques from Topographic maps, proposed in research work [13]. Topographic maps are currently used by Geographic Information Systems (GIS) professionals in the graphical visualisation of features of land surfaces to understand depths, valleys, and terrains using colour mapping and contours.

[1] https://www.wired.com/story/alphv-change-healthcare-ransomware-payment/.

TAM-based visualisation, allows attribute (feature) classification while also preserving the graph structure. This allows the users to analyse a dataset from two different perspectives: the topological perspective, which focuses on the physical structure of the graph built on the interactions, and the attribute-based perspective, which focuses on grouping nodes based on a particular feature. Further, the visualisation use cases reported by Preiner et al. in [13] evidence the data anomaly detection ability of TAM in many domains; the applications including network traffic analysis, node space coverage for software code repositories, ancestral graphs, and densely connected graphs. Considering its key properties and tested use cases, TAM may be proposed as an excellent graphical representation method that resolves some of the key limitation in the attributed graph-based visualisation of blockchain transaction data stated above. The malicious activities in blockchain networks involve a collection of interactions between wallets. The properties of TAM facilitate positioning the wallets based on the similarities and classifying them via various colour shades.

This technique being a recent proposal, has not yet been applied to other domains apart from the test cases in the original paper [13]. Further, even though graphical techniques like attributed graphs have been used for blockchain data visualisation, the approach in TAM is a novel method for this application. Considering these benefits, this paper proposes a novel approach for TAM-based visualisation for blockchain transactions. The proposed approach utilises attributed graph data of the blockchain transactions and then provides three different views based on the nodes, links (edges between nodes), and the properties of TAM. The main contributions of this work are:

- Proposed TAM-based visualisation approach for blockchain-attributed graph
- Proposed to develop a methodology for transforming blockchain graph data to visualise the similarity and link force-based features of TAM
- Evaluated the proposed approach using phishing settlement-related Ethereum transactions.

The paper is structured as follows. Section 2 presents related work for blockchain transaction data visualisation. Section 3 documents the proposed methodology for proposed TAM-based visualisation for blockchain transactions. Section 4 provides results and evaluation for phishing settlement-related Ethereum network transaction data. Section 5 provides a critical discussion of the findings. Section 6 concludes with the findings while presenting future work based on the proposed approach.

2 Literature Review

Several works have been carried out previously related to Blockchain technology and its applications. Most of the applications are intended to eliminate the need for manual touch-points in networks, increase security, or enhance convenience. For example, Xu et al. [20] proposed a blockchain-based data auditing framework as a solution for reliability issues in traditional storage methods. The authors developed a smart contract that enabled the remote auditing service of data. Another blockchain-based methodology was proposed by Dorri et al. [6] to ensure privacy and security in an Internet of Things (IoT) network. This approach to blockchain aimed to eliminate the high processing power required for traditional consensus mechanism Proof of Work (PoW). Hence, the authors proposed a lightweight blockchain framework specifically tailored for a smart home concept. This aimed to provide efficiency and robust security with minimal overhead. These works improved the performance of traditional methods but did not address the issues related to the potential threat of malicious transactions.

Analysis of blockchain transactions has also been a considerable scholarly topic. Baran et al. [10] discussed the importance of graph analysis of blockchain data. The paper emphasized the current risks posed by blockchain transactions, using recent incidents involved. They provided a comprehensive overview of the vulnerabilities in blockchain networks that are being exploited by the attackers. As a solution to address these issues, the paper proposed a blockchain transaction graph analysis system. This proposed system was supported by results obtained from running a set of parallel graph algorithms on large-scale real Bitcoin and Ethereum blockchain data.

Many works emphasized the effectiveness of visualisation techniques to aid in handling these types of complex data to reach meaningful insights. Tharani et al. [15] explained how decentralization and pseudo-anonymity in public blockchains can lead to fraudulent transactions. The authors demonstrated how the traditional auditing techniques may fail in detecting these activities as the complexity of blockchains may require higher processing capability and time. The article, thus, proposed a set of algorithms to extract features from blockchain-based transactions to represent the data graphically. This was intended to reflect anomalies using graphical visualisation [15].

Preiner et al. [13] proposed a novel form of data visualisation called the Topographic Attribute Maps. The authors explained how the two types of graphs: topological graphs, and attribute-based graphs collide when trying to visualize data using different features. TAM offers both these abilities, by supporting the graph's topological structure while also enabling classification using a certain attribute in visualisation. The authors introduced an open-source tool to develop this map by importing a dataset in JSON format. This work aimed to improve the convenience of handling complex data.

Although many works have been carried out in the areas of blockchain technology, blockchain data visualisation, and analysing malicious activities in blockchain networks, TAM has not yet been applied to visualise malicious transactions in blockchain networks. This article addresses this research gap by presenting a method that tailors both TAM and blockchain data so that this data can be properly visualised to uncover malicious behaviour patterns in blockchain networks. This technique will offer numerous benefits to blockchain transaction analysis such as easy understanding without expertise knowlege, clear visualisations concerning interactions as well as a chosen characteristic, and the ability to analyse using different characteristics separately.

3 Methodology

This section details the methodology of the proposed approach to visualise blockchain transactions using TAM. Figure 1 illustrates five phases of the proposed methodology: data collection from public blockchains, data pre-processing, attributed graph construction for blockchain transactions (graph modelling), data normalisation for TAM representation, and finally TAM-based visualisation. The following subsections describe each phase in detail.

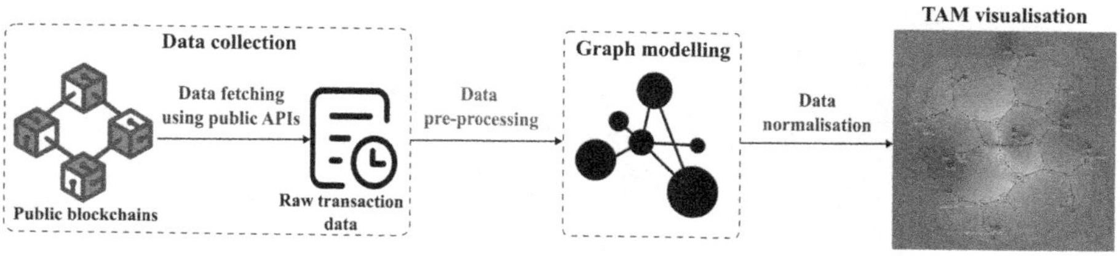

Fig. 1. Proposed methodology for TAM-based visualisation.

3.1 Data Collection and Pre-processing

This paper considered normal and phishing settlement-related Externally Owned Accounts (EOAs) as a case study for TAM visualisation. An EOA is an account type, that provides direct blockchain network access and allows users to send transactions directly via them [14]. Data collection used public API[2] in obtaining transaction details for given EOA addresses in the JSON format. In the pre-processing phase, null transactions and transactions with invalid status are removed. The pre-processed data is then considered for feature extraction. The structural features of EOA are extracted from raw transaction data using the approach proposed in [16]. The EOAs in the collected dataset are labelled based on the published "First-order Transaction Network of Phishing Nodes" [18] dataset.

3.2 Graph Modeling

Topographic Attribute Maps only support static visualisations. Considering this limitation, the graph modelling phase converts the raw EOAs transaction data into Money Flow Transaction (MFT) graph G [15]. In the graph, $G = (V, E)$ vertices V represent the set of EOAs and edges $E \subseteq V \times V$ represent the set of transactions between EOAs. Each EOA has a set of features. Each edge $e(u, v)$ represents the amount of Ether transferred between EOAs u and v based on the algorithm proposed in [15]. Figure 2 illustrates a money flow transaction graph related to phishing settlement. Visualising an attributed graph of the blockchain network into TAM needs a specific transformation. This transformation is detailed in the following data normalisation subsection.

[2] https://api.blockcypher.com/v1/eth/main/addrs/.

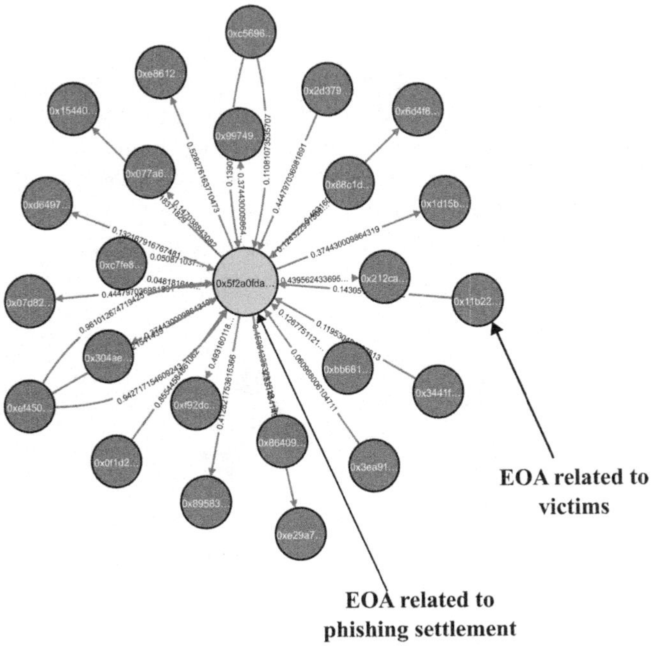

Fig. 2. Money flow transaction graph for EOAs related to phishing settlement.

3.3 Data Normalisation

Data normalisation handles the graph data of the blockchain network obtained from graph modelling, converting it into the format required by the proposed TAM algorithm. This format is a list of 'nodes' and 'links' represented as JSON objects.

Each 'node' should have three keys: "id", "name" and "value" as shown in the example below. Here, "id" is the node's identifier, "name" is the node's label that will be displayed on the map, and "value" is the value of the chosen attribute used for visualisation.

```
{
    "id": "1",
    "name": "0x760a412a14f2fe03c0873b473febdf79db288fce",
    "value": 2
}
```

It is important to mention here that TAM-based visualisation only allows data to be visualised based on a single attribute at a time. It would also be valid if the "value" key includes values from different attributes in an array, as shown below (in the example, `node.value[0]` refers to the Ether value, while `node.value[1]` refers to the year of the transaction). However, in this case, it is still needed to specify which attribute to use for the visualisation.

```
{
    "id": "1",
    "name": "0x760a412a14f2fe03c0873b473febdf79db288fce",
    "value" : [0.00019464, 2016]
}
```

In this paper, we use the single value format and experiment with three different attributes: the Ether amount, number of receiving transactions (indegree), and number of sending transactions(outdegree) of an EOA separately.

The fact that the TAM-based visualisation is based on a single attribute value only may be considered as a limitation; However, in this paper, we utilised this to compare the TAMs generated for indegree and outdegree properties of the EOA. The TAM for blockchain network can be generated for the aggregated features or network property-based features of EOA or smart contract or the wallet [16].

As mentioned above, the required format also includes 'links' objects. Each 'link' represents the connection between two nodes. A 'link' object should include three keys: "source", "target" and "directed". "source" and "target" are the identification numbers of the two connected nodes, and a boolean type key "directed" indicates whether the link is directed or not, as shown in the example below.

```
{
    "source": "51082",
    "target": "81484",
    "directed": true
}
```

The outcome of the data normalisation considered for the proposed TAM visualisation is explained in the following subsection.

3.4 TAM-Based Visualisation

In this paper, we propose applying a TAM-based visualisation approach to the graph structure of the blockchain network's transaction data. The proposed method can also be applied to the transaction graph of the Bitcoin network and the address graph of both the Bitcoin and Ethereum networks.

A well-known technique for the visualisation of blockchain transaction data is attributed graph-based visualisation. One limitation of this technique is the lack of classifying nodes based on their characteristics. Classifying based on a certain characteristic facilitates better data visualisation, making it easier for analysts to spot patterns and trends that might indicate suspicious activity. This is an important feature when considering illegal activity detection. Further, the attributed graph with complex data might result in overlapping nodes and links. In this paper, we utilise TAM properties of forces and colour mapping to tackle the limitation in classification. Further, TAM as a force-directed graph, incorporates two measures of forces between the nodes to render the visualisation, while minimising node overlapping. In a force-directed graph, the node interactions simulate forces in metal coil springs. The forces indicate attractions and repulsions similar to that of physical springs. The forces between the similar nodes are called the "Similarity forces" (F_s), while the forces between the linked nodes are called the "Link forces" (F_l). In this application, F_s are applied between the nodes depicting the similar-valued EOAs, and F_l are applied between the linked EOAs. These two forces support maintaining the graph in equilibrium [8]. The equation corresponding to the similarity force is mentioned below.

$$F_s(i,j) = \|x_i - x_j\| \tag{1}$$

The similarity force F_s is calculated based on the magnitude difference between the attribute values x_i, x_j of nodes i, and j in the attributed graph. Similarity forces are the forces exerted on nodes with similar attributes. This force is responsible for supporting nodes with similar or closely related attributes to be placed together. Figure 3 (a) and (b) show the difference in the TAM visualisation using different F_s values on the same data set.

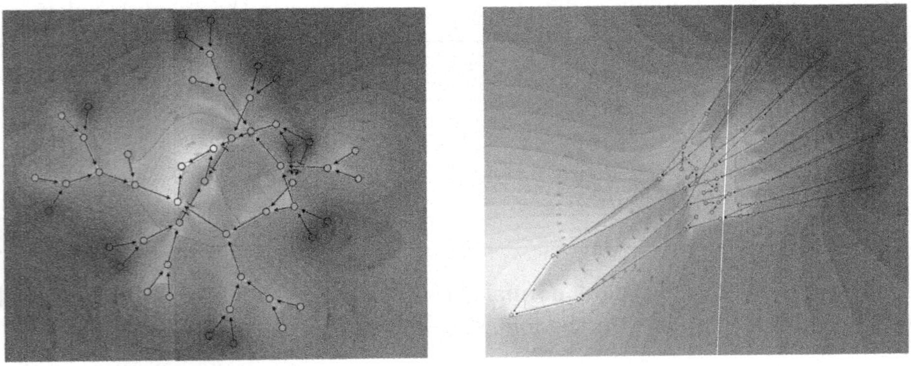

(a) Similarity force = 0 (default) **(b) Similarity force = 0.4**

Fig. 3. Influence of similarity force in TAM.

If the graph only consists of similarity forces, the nodes are likely to overlap with each other. The link forces/link strengths are introduced to the force-directed graphs to prevent overlapping. Link forces acts as repulsive forces that push linked nodes away from each other. These forces balance the graph by minimising the influence of the similarity force, by converting the graph more toward a proper topological layout. The equation corresponding to the Link force is mentioned below.

$$F_l(i) = \frac{|V_i|}{|S_i|} \tag{2}$$

Here, the link force F_l is calculated using two parameters. $|V_i|$ is the number of nodes connected with the target node. This work calculates the link force using the number of spending and receiving transactions of the given EOA. $|S_i|$ is the number of virtual springs affected due to the similarity force F_s. Figure 4 (a) and (b) show F_l based visualisation with the different values as link strengths. These figures indicate how the end nodes or the edges (non-linked nodes) are placed further from each other as the link strength has decreased from the first instance to the second.

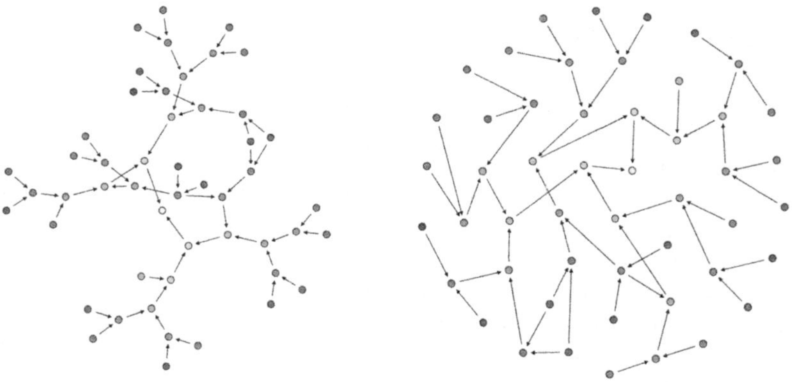

(a) Link strength = 0.8 (default) **(b) Link strength = 0**

Fig. 4. Influence of link strengths in TAM.

Another factor in the TAM-based visualisation is that the values of the selected attribute of all the nodes in the input data need to fall within a certain range to produce informative outcomes, such as clusters of nodes and contours.

In the process of generating TAM, the values from all the nodes are stored in a set M. The *range* is defined by the minimum and maximum values in M, i.e. $range = (M_{min}, M_{max})$. This range is then split into C_n equal intervals, and a colour shade is assigned to each interval based on the range and the average of the values as a midpoint (for more information on this process refer [2]). Nodes are coloured in TAM based on the interval their value is in, as shown in Fig. 5. It is easy to see that the distribution of values within the range may affect the resulting TAM.

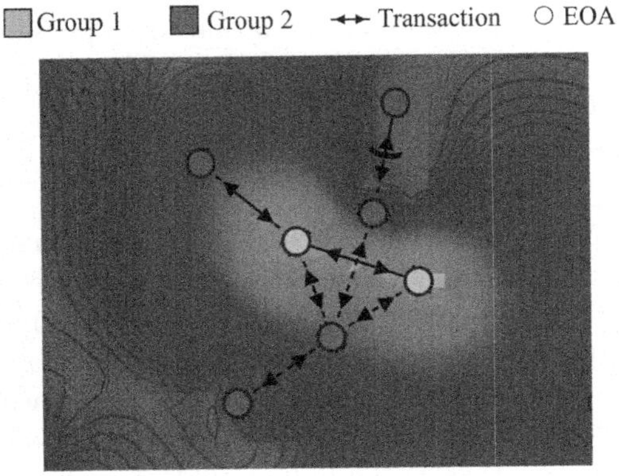

Fig. 5. TAM visualisation for sample Ether data.

4 Results and Evaluation

This section details the results of the proposed TAM-based visualisation using the case study related to phishing settlement-based illegal activities in the Ethereum network. The labels of the phishing and normal EOAs were obtained from the published data repository [18]. The attributed graph of the Ethereum network is considered for the visualisation. Here nodes are the EOAs and the links are the transactions between EOAs. The TAM-based visualisation was tested for three EOA properties: the amount of Ether transferred within EOAs, indegree, and outdegree values from the money flow transaction graph. These were gathered into three separate datasets in JSON format, and fed into the open-source TAM tool proposed by [13], for visualisation.

4.1 Visualisation Based on the Amount of Ether

TAM-based visualisation for the original (un-normalised) transaction amount properties is shown in Fig. 6. The original values of the transaction amount were extremely low and fell within an interval of 0 to 1×10^{-13}. However, the majority of node values were 2.1×10^{-14}. As shown in Fig. 6 the original range of values placed the EOAs in similar colours (Group 1), and no colour shades could be seen to classify the data according to their value. This is due to the algorithm logic used in mapping the values, to the colour shades. As the values in the original dataset are distributed within a narrow range, these values do not properly map to distinctive colour shades, hence do not provide a clear TAM generation. Therefore, it is required to bring the original values to a suitable range supported by this mapping. Therefore, the original outcome was improved by multiplying all Ether values by 10^{17}. The new values resulted in approximately between 0 and 10,000. For this new range, four major clusters were identified in TAM, each for groups of nodes with values around 0.001, 2100, 5000, and 10,000. The normalised TAM-based visualisation for these four clusters is presented in Fig. 7.

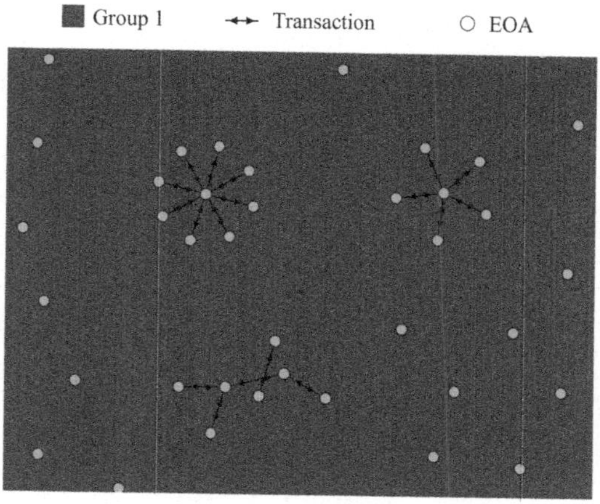

Fig. 6. TAM visualisation for the original data.

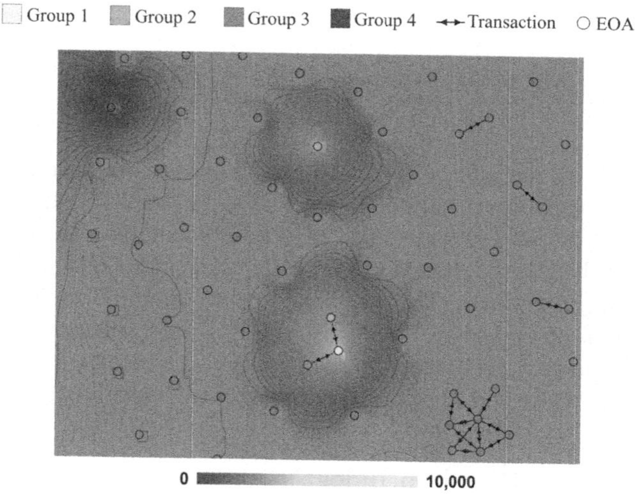

Fig. 7. TAM visualisation for the normalised data.

The identified clusters were compared with the original labels identified from the XBlock phishing dataset [18]. Based on the observation, the majority of the nodes were grouped in the range of 2100–2108. Only a few EOAs belonged to the range of 2109 to 10,000, which was a count of 20 out of the total 568 nodes. Further, the value differences between nodes in the range 2100–2108 could not be observed in the TAM due to the higher values. This is due to TAM's algorithm for generating the colour map based on the minimum value, maximum value and midpoint. As the minimum and maximum values for the range are 0.01, and 10,000 respectively, the 2100–2108 difference had been considered negligible and hence all the nodes in this range are placed in the same shade.

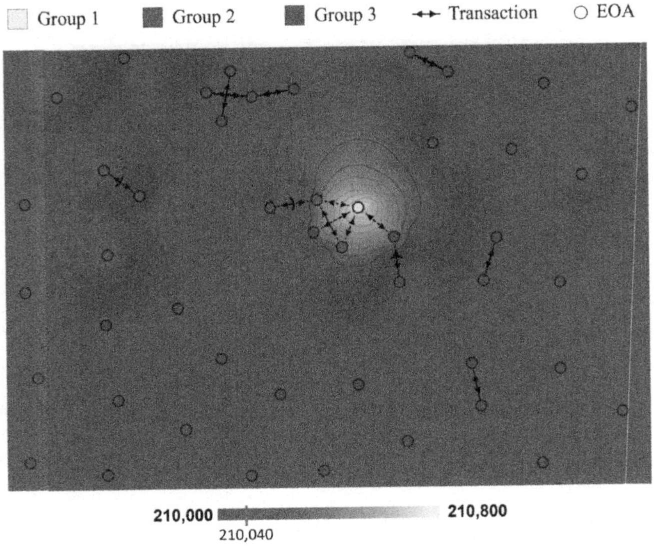

Fig. 8. TAM visualisation for the filtered data.

After observing the outcome of this TAM-based visualisation, this minority was removed, to visualise the anomalies within the 2100–2108 range clearly. Next, these filtered values were considered for the data normalisation. During the data normalisation, the filtered values were once again multiplied by 100, to improve the values in decimal places. This normalised data outcome could visualise three colour groups as presented in Fig. 8. The results were then compared with the actual list of phishing settlement-related EOAs. Out of the 18 EOAs, 16 were visualised in TAM as anomalies. The accuracy of the visualisation is nearly 84%.

4.2 Visualisation Based on Indegree and Outdegree

The indegree of the EOA reflects the number of receiving transactions and outdegree reflects the number of sending transactions. Figure 9 (a) and (b) present TAM-based visualisation results for indegree and outdegree features of the EOA, respectively. In the experimental dataset, indegree and outdegree values ranged between 1–30. The EOAs in the lightest blue regions are correlated with the normal labels, moderately light blue regions are correlated with the phishing labels, and in the darker regions is a mix of normal (50) and phishing EOAs (94). The challenge on this is distinguishing indegree and outdegree values of EOAs in the darker regions as normal and phishing via TAM-based visualisation.

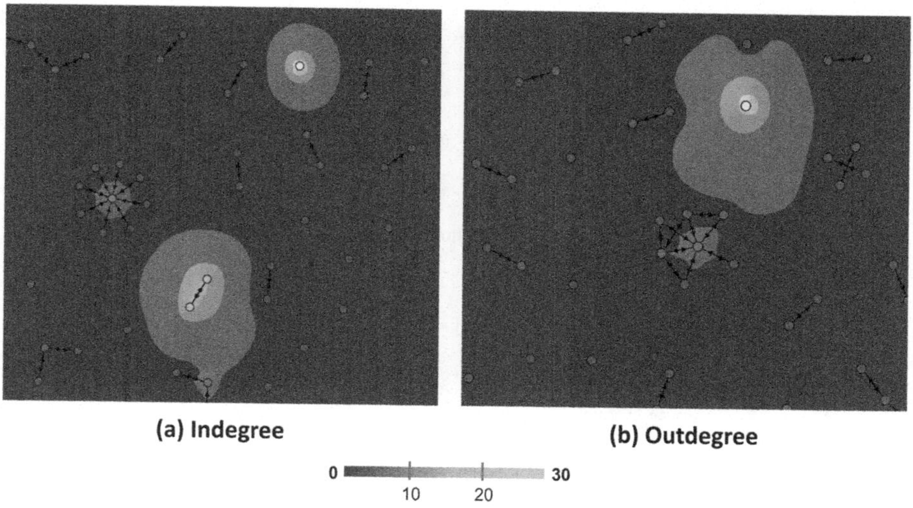

Fig. 9. TAM visualisation for transaction degree.

5 Discussion

This section discusses the benefits and limitations of TAM-based visualisation. Figure 10 represents the attributed graph for the normal and phishing settlement-related EOAs. This visualisation only presents how EOAs are interconnected via a transaction link between them. The TAM-based visualisation for the same data presented in Fig. 5 and Fig. 9, enhance the attributed graph visualisation by grouping the nodes based on their similarities, drawing a boundary (contour) for each group, and giving a different shade of colour for the groups. This colour shades and contours offer an interactive and distinctive visualisation of anomalies, which can be easily observed without any expertise knowledge. These properties of TAM-based visualisation are beneficial for end users such as forensic analysers, financial regulators, and legal authorities to identify the group of EOAs/wallets/smart contracts related to illegal financial activities such as money laundering, ransomware settlements, Ponzi schemes, and scams for their decision making. Further, the colour-coded pictures of the TAM can be utilised as an informative digital footprint for the investigations.

5.1 Limitations

One limitation of the proposed TAM-based visualisation is the requirement of high processing power when handling large datasets and data with high values. This causes a small delay when generating the graph and generating the colour shades. Another limitation is the requirement of precise data tailoring before uploading them to the TAM which is highly dependent on different ranges in the node property values. The colour and contour generation of the TAM process is based on these ranges. The absence of a defined approach for the normalisation

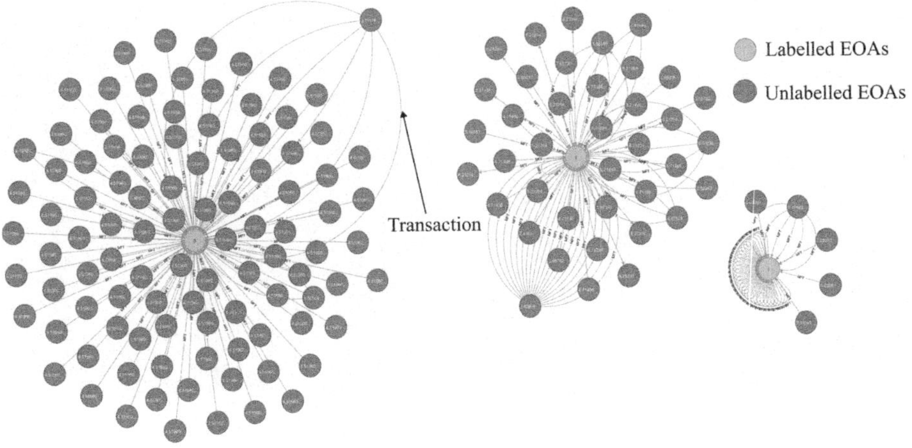

Fig. 10. Attributed graph for experimental data.

is considered a limitation. Further, the proposed TAM requires the type of node to be similar to the attributed graph. For instance, if the attributed graph has both EOA and transaction as nodes, the proposed TAM-based visualisation does not provide a meaningful outcome. In this case, all the nodes should either be EOA or transactions. Another limitation is that the current TAM version only supports a fixed dataset and therefore does not support dynamic data analysis. The experiments conducted for TAM-based visualization utilized static transaction data stored on the local machine. The efficiency of the proposed analysis was not evaluated using dynamic data streaming from a public blockchain network.

6 Conclusion and Future Work

This research has demonstrated the benefits of TAM-based visualisation in the analysis of blockchain networks to identify suspicious activities. The results of the TAM for three different properties of EOAs illustrate both challenging and distinguishable ranges of these properties via grouping and colouring. The mapping between the EOAs and their Ether values in TAM-based visualisation and their original labels reveals that 84% of the phishing settlement-related EOAs were shaded within a similar colour shade and the same contour, thereby being visualised as anomalies. The future work of the proposed approach aims to improve this method to classify data using more than one attribute, and extending the proposed methodology to other critical infrastructures.

The proposed system lays the foundation for future work. Currently, TAM provides meaningful insights for nodes and links being on the same domain. A suggested enhancement would be to improve the mechanism to support nodes and links of multiple domains simultaneously. Further, as the proposed method only supports static data analysis, another potential future research area would be to improve this method to support dynamic data analysis.

References

1. Bitcoininfor (2024). https://bitinfocharts.com/
2. D3.js (2024). https://d3js.org/d3-scale/diverging
3. Etherscan (2024). https://etherscan.io/
4. Infura (2024). https://www.infura.io/
5. Bistarelli, S., Santini, F.: Go with the-bitcoin-flow, with visual analytics. In: Proceedings of the 12th International Conference on Availability, Reliability and Security, pp. 1–6 (2017)
6. Dorri, A., Kanhere, S.S., Jurdak, R., Gauravaram, P.: Blockchain for iot security and privacy: the case study of a smart home. In: 2017 IEEE International Conference on Pervasive Computing and Communications Workshops (PerCom Workshops), pp. 618–623 (2017). https://doi.org/10.1109/PERCOMW.2017.7917634
7. Framewala, A., Harale, S., Khatal, S., Patel, D., Busnel, Y., Rajarajan, M.: Blockchain analysis tool for monitoring coin flow. In: 2020 Seventh International Conference on Software Defined Systems (SDS), pp. 196–201. IEEE (2020)
8. Fruchterman, T.M.J., Reingold, E.M.: Graph drawing by force-directed placement. Softw. Pract. Exp. **21** (1991). https://api.semanticscholar.org/CorpusID:31468174
9. Jeyakumar, S.T., Ko, R., Muthukkumarasamy, V.: A framework for user-centric visualisation of blockchain transactions in critical infrastructure. In: Proceedings of the 5th ACM International Symposium on Blockchain and Secure Critical Infrastructure, BSCI '23, pp. 44–52. Association for Computing Machinery, New York (2023). https://doi.org/10.1145/3594556.3594624
10. Kılıç, B., Özturan, C., Şen, A.: Analyzing large-scale blockchain transaction graphs for fraudulent activities, pp. 253–267. Springer, Cham (2022). https://doi.org/10.1007/978-3-030-94590-9_14
11. Nakamoto, S.: Bitcoin: a peer-to-peer electronic cash system (2008)
12. Peters, G., Panayi, E., Chapelle, A.: Trends in crypto-currencies and blockchain technologies: a monetary theory and regulation perspective. SSRN Electron. J. (2015). https://doi.org/10.2139/ssrn.2646618
13. Preiner, R., Schmidt, J., Krösl, K., Schreck, T., Mistelbauer, G.: Augmenting node-link diagrams with topographic attribute maps. Comput. Graph. Forum **39** (2020). https://doi.org/10.1111/cgf.13987
14. Rouhani, S., Deters, R.: Performance analysis of ethereum transactions in private blockchain. In: 2017 8th IEEE International Conference on Software Engineering and Service Science (ICSESS), pp. 70–74 (2017). https://doi.org/10.1109/ICSESS.2017.8342866
15. Tharani, J.S., Charles, E.Y.A., Hóu, Z., Palaniswami, M., Muthukkumarasamy, V.: Graph based visualisation techniques for analysis of blockchain transactions. In: 2021 IEEE 46th Conference on Local Computer Networks (LCN), pp. 427–430 (2021). https://doi.org/10.1109/LCN52139.2021.9524878
16. Tharani, J.S., Hóu, Z., Charles, E.Y.A., Rathore, P., Palaniswami, M., Muthukkumarasamy, V.: Unified feature engineering for detection of malicious entities in blockchain networks. IEEE Trans. Inf. Forensics Secur. (2024). https://doi.org/10.1109/TIFS.2024.3412421
17. Tsoulias, K., Palaiokrassas, G., Fragkos, G., Litke, A., Varvarigou, T.A.: A graph model based blockchain implementation for increasing performance and security in decentralized ledger systems. IEEE Access **8**, 130952–130965 (2020)
18. Wu, J., et al.: Who are the phishers? Phishing scam detection on ethereum via network embedding. IEEE Trans. Syst. Man Cybern. Syst. **52**(2), 1156–1166 (2022). https://doi.org/10.1109/TSMC.2020.3016821

19. Wu, Y., Luo, A., Xu, D.: Identifying suspicious addresses in bitcoin thefts. Digit. Invest. **31**, 200895 (2019)
20. Xu, Y., Ren, J., Zhang, Y., Zhang, C., Shen, B., Zhang, Y.: Blockchain empowered arbitrable data auditing scheme for network storage as a service. IEEE Trans. Serv. Comput. **13**(2), 289–300 (2020). https://doi.org/10.1109/TSC.2019.2953033
21. Zheng, Z., Xie, S., Dai, H., Chen, X., Wang, H.: An overview of blockchain technology: architecture, consensus, and future trends. In: 2017 IEEE International Congress on Big Data (BigData Congress), pp. 557–564 (2017). https://doi.org/10.1109/BigDataCongress.2017.85

Tokenized Property Renting and Trading Using Blockchain

Md. Miraj Hossain, Md Yeasin Ali, Tasmia Akand, Senjuti Saha, Kazi Sazid Ahmed, Kazi Tasmima Eshan, and Md Sadek Ferdous(✉)

Brac University, Dhaka, Bangladesh
{md.miraj.hossain,tasmia.akand,senjuti.saha,kazi.sazid.ahmed, kazi.tasmima.eshan}@g.bracu.ac.bd, {yeasin.ali,sadek.ferdous}@bracu.ac.bd

Abstract. Managing the extensive house rental market is a challenging task for authorities, mainly due to the numerous landlords, arbitrary fees, misleading rental details, and related complexities. To address these issues, this paper introduces a property transaction and rental system based on Blockchain and NFTs. The system utilizes smart contracts to represent various agreements, establish relationships among users, automatically pay and collect rent regularly, and return rental rights upon expiration. This system eliminates the need for mediation, reduces costs, ensures transparency in rental information, and simplifies record-keeping for authorities. In this paper, we present the system architecture based on a threat model and different requirements, discuss the implementation of a Proof-of-Concept, present the system use-cases and subsequent protocol flows. Finally, we analyze the defined security and functional requirements, the expected cost to use the system, and highlight the different advantages and disadvantages of the system.

Keywords: Blockchain · Tokenization · Smart Contract · NFT · Real Estate

1 Introduction

Since ancient times, housing has been a fundamental necessity for humans. The increase in population and urbanization has turned rental housing into a daunting facet of modern living. In conjunction with a growing population, the size of the rental real estate industry has increased significantly. The amount is expected to expand significantly at a compound annual growth rate of 7.5%, from the current estimation of 2806.83 billion USD (US$s) in 2024 to 3,749.95 billion USD in 2028 [14]. Currently, one of the significant rental service modes is online-based, which was predicted to have a market worth of 18.24 billion USD, and by 2033, the value is projected to have increased by 77.09 billion USD [2]. Considering the growth rate and to gain trust from clients, conventional rental systems require special attention, as these systems often result in fraudulent activities [16,25] and cause inconveniences for both property owners and renters [37], thus

S. Kanhere et al. (Eds.): SDLT 2024, CCIS 2453, pp. 19–37, 2025.
https://doi.org/10.1007/978-981-96-4442-1_2

worsening the problem. As per a report published in 2020 during the COVID pandemic [28], property managers indicate that 15% of online rental applications show clear fraud, with an additional 10% going unreported. These issues lead to various negative consequences such as property damage, missed opportunities, alleged crimes, and reputational damage for owners.

This is still on the rise, and a new report says 93.3% of 75 owner, developer and manager respondents experienced fraud within 12 months in 2023 [23]. Accepting cash payments raises fraud concerns, manual record-keeping, and receipt management issues, potentially leading to rent disputes and exposing landlords to robbery as physical cash management is cumbersome and can be traced by individuals with ill intent [24,31]. Moreover, on the tenants' side, concerns encompass wrongful evictions due to owners' self-interest or nepotism [22], unauthorized rent increases [33] and illegitimate multi-month advance rent demands. This research aims to address these issues by leveraging Blockchain technology, specifically NFTs, to build a new user-friendly and transparent system.

Blockchain is a popular choice for secure and transparent distributed ledger systems. Our proposed system uses non-fungible tokens (NFTs) to tokenize assets, ensuring exclusivity and non-duplicability of real estate assets. This paper aims to design a user-friendly, secure, cost-efficient and transparent online property purchase and renting system for flats or single rooms. The system is faster, simpler, and cheaper in addressing different limitations of traditional systems.

Contributions: The major contributions of this paper are:

- Proposing an automated platform to manage the processes of buying, selling, and renting.
- We explain the motivation of the system and discuss its architecture that addresses different security threats and present various functional and security requirements.
- We define detailed protocol flows involving different use-cases of the system.
- We discuss how the system satisfies different formulated requirements.
- Finally, we discuss the advantages and limitations of our system.

Structure: Sect. 2 introduces different background topics and Sect. 3 reviews related research. Different assumed threats and functional and security requirements are described in Sect. 4. The architecture and its implementation are presented in Sect. 5. Different use-cases with the respective protocol flows are discussed in Sect. 6. We analyze the associated cost of using the system, compare it with existing platforms and discuss its advantages and limitations in Sect. 7. Finally, we conclude in Sect. 8.

2 Background

In this section, we briefly discuss about Blockchain (Sect. 2.1), Ethereum platform (Sect. 2.2) and Tokenization (Sect. 2.3).

2.1 Blockchain

Blockchain has the potential to offer a secure, decentralized asset ownership tracking [39] and can be an excellent solution in real estate transactions ensuring trust and transparency of data [29]. It uses a shared database with cryptographic links between data blocks, making it tamper-proof and publicly visible [27]. It is a decentralized system, managed by multiple users across various nodes which records transactions using cryptographic mechanisms ensuring higher protection.

2.2 Ethereum and Smart Contacts

Ethereum is the first smart-contract supported decentralized blockchain system [6]. These smart contracts represent applications that operate autonomously based on predefined rules and data stored at specific addresses on the Ethereum blockchain. The autonomous nature and immutability of completed transactions make Ethereum's smart contracts one of the most trustworthy and secure technologies currently available.

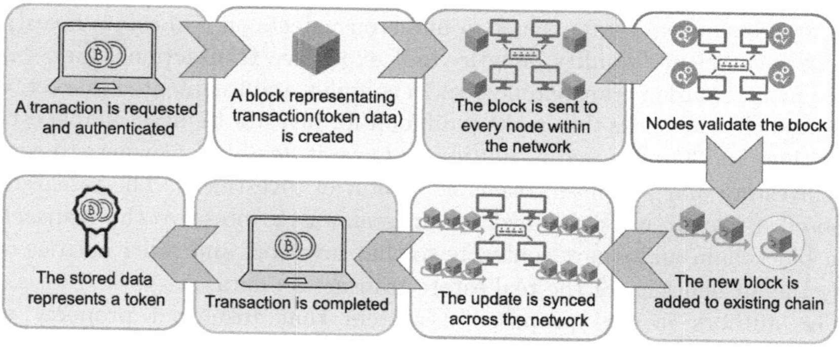

Fig. 1. Tokenization Process

2.3 Tokenization

A token is a digital representation of an asset on a blockchain, similar to a security document, and is technically a standard implemented with the help of a smart Contract [43]. The asset can be digital or physical. There are two types of tokens: Fungible Tokens and Non-fungible tokens (NFTs). Fungible tokens are digital assets with identical value and interchangeability, and can be closely related to a fiat currency, traditional finance, and economics, while a non-fungible token can be represented as a unique one-of-a-kind digital asset [8]. A blockchain transaction (Fig. 1) guarantees that once someone owns a token representing an asset, none can tamper that ownership, making it entirely immutable. Different thins, such as paintings, digital media platforms, real estates, company shares, or collectibles, can be tokenized on a distributed ledger [20]. Tokenization can bring benefits to the asset owners in terms of increased liquidity, fair price, reduced management cost, composability, accessibility, transparency and easy tradability [4,20]. In simple words, tokenization in real estate and rental can be referred to as the digital representation of data which traces the unique ownership and renting information through blockchain which is completely tamper-resistant.

3 Related Work

In recent years, researchers have emphasized different aspects of the real estate systems leveraging blockchain and tokenizations.

Spielman et al. compared the blockchain-based system architecture with existing systems and discussed different advantages and drawbacks [41]. Konashevych et al. extended the research by examining the capabilities of blockchain and DLTs and their suitability for different applications in real estate [34]. Even countries like Dubai [5], Sweden [26] have already experimented with blockchain in land registration or real estate projects due to its potential.

In a study [35], the authors stated the heterogeneity and immobility as the main features of real estate that had numerous effects on real estate investment such as insufficient liquidity, lengthy and expensive transactions, high capital requirements, market transparency, and a complex and fragmented market. Considering such drawbacks that make it difficult for investor to invest in real estates, the authors in [30] proposed a solution to make it flexible for owners to connect with investors and purchase tokens as a form of investment. The research [44] proposed a similar work, however, their goal was to preserve the transactions using blockchain and smart contracts so that investors and other entities could verify the authenticity of the real estate transaction data.

The authors in [38] proposed a system that tokenized property using Ethereum and smart contracts to enhance the ownership transfer process. The work focused on eradicating fraud and eliminating the challenges associated with verifying the identity of the authentic property owner. Similarly, Thosar et al. [42] focused on the ownership transfer and registration of properties using blockchain. Focusing on tokenization, the authors in [32,36] proposed different approaches to tokenize assets and properties to manage ownership and its transfer process.

These studies attempted to leverage blockchains and some of them tokenized properties; however, one important aspect missing in these works is freedom of renting only a portion of a property or flat. In addition, these studies lacked proper functional and security requirements and detailed a protocol design. Many of these studies only presented ideas without any implementation.

4 Threat Model and System Requirements

In this section, we define some threats (Sect. 4.1) and explore different system requirements for the proposed system (Sect. 4.2).

4.1 Threat Modeling

In order to model threats, we utilize the STRIDE framework [40]. Additionally, we consider the reply attack as it is a common threat in a blockchain-based system with the possibility of double spending. The threats are briefly discussed below.

T1. **Spoofing:** A spoofing attack implies that an attacker impersonates someone or something by falsifying data.
T2. **Tampering:** This attack undermines the integrity of data by altering it with malicious intent.
T3. **Repudiation:** This risk signifies that a user has the ability to refute actions, and the system lacks the means to challenge this incorrect assertion.
T4. **Information Disclosure:** This threat signifies unintentional data leak.
T5. **Denial of Service (DoS):** An attack that overwhelms a service with an excessive number of malicious requests, rendering it unavailable.
T6. **Elevation of Privilege:** This threat implies that an attacker uses different attack vectors of an application to gain unauthorized accesses to resources. This is out of our research scope as it requires employing additional access control mechanisms which we have not considered.
T7. **Reply Attack:** This threat implies that an attacker may capture a request or response which will be resent later on to execute the same action twice.

4.2 Requirement Analysis

In the following we consider various functional and security requirements.

Functional Requirements: The functional requirements are presented next.

FR1. It should be a platform where the owner can offer to rent their flats and the renter can easily get those rentable flats.
FR2. The users should be able to create a profile id with valid information to retrieve a unique user id.
FR3. The system should be integrated with a decentralized infrastructure so that the system cannot be controlled by a person or a group of people.
FR4. It should have a peer-to-peer transaction system.
FR5. It should have a tokenization system where the user or the owner can tokenize their property.
FR6. The system should facilitate trust by ensuring that transactions are transparent and immutable.

Security Requirements. The security requirements that we consider prior to design the systems are listed next.

SR1. The application must be implemented with a strong authentication mechanism to mitigate the *T1* threat.
SR2. The application should ensure the integrity of the stored data to mitigate *T2*.
SR3. The application should utilise digital signature to mitigate any repudiation attack (*T3*).
SR4. All the sensitive data should be encrypted during transmission to mitigate *T4*.
SR5. It is desirable for the system to employ mechanisms to mitigate *T5*.
SR6. The system should enforce protective mechanisms to prevent *T7* so that no double spending occurs.

5 Architecture and Implementation

In this section, we discuss the architecture and implementation details of the system.

5.1 Architecture

The system facilitates a website that lists different properties. When a user wants to buy, sell or rent a property, they must register themselves as a seller (owner of a property), a buyer or a renter by providing valid information. Once registered, users can create a new token of their owned property and list it in the system for renters or buyers. When a user rents or buys the property, the token metadata gets updated according to the updated data. To get these services, users interact with our system through a browser. The high-level architecture of the system is presented in Fig. 2. The architecture has three important components, DApp (Decentralized App), IPFS (InterPlanetary File System) and a Blockchain system, which are discussed below.

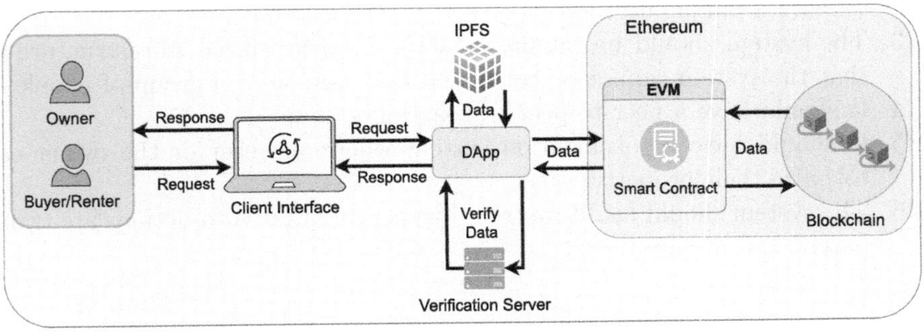

Fig. 2. High-level Architecture of the System

DApp: The DApp is a distributed, decentralized, open-source software program that acts as the middleware between in the user browser, IPFS and the Blockchain. It provides a website which acts as the user interface for any user to tokenize their property in this system. Users can sign up or in using their information using this interface. A user will also have a specific profile, be able to examine their history, update their information, and give rent, among other services using this interface. This DApp also enables to the user to interact with the IPFS and the corresponding smart contract of the blockchain platform. The DApp also depends on a verification server to verify the authenticity of user's information as well as to verify the information regarding a property. It is assumed that the identity verification server is maintained by the Government of a country and hence, is not discussed any further.

IPFS: Interplanetary File System [21] is a distributed file storage protocol that allows for fast performance and decentralized data archiving. Moreover, the IPFS protocol automatically generates a hash value of the stored data which is later used to to retrieve such data. In our system, we have used IPFS to store comparatively less sensitive data (e.g. property pictures, price lists and so on) as they could consume huge storage space and it will be very expensive to store such data in a blockchain.

Blockchain: For the system, we have used Ethereum [6] which is a smart-contract supported public blockchain system. The smart-contract platform enables the creation of different types of tokens. Even though there are many different smart-contract supporting public blockchain systems (e.g. Solana [17] and Cardano [19], however, Ethereum is the most popular one.

5.2 Implementation

To develop the system, we have used ReactJS [13] and Tailwind CSS [18] for the front-end UI and NodeJS [11] to develop the DApp and Solidity to develop the respective smart contract [6]. Moreover, we have used the ERC721 [7] standard to tokenize each property in the form of Non-Fungible Tokens (NFTs) which represent the ownership of a property by a certain user. We have also used Hardhat [10] as a development environment and Goreli which is a Proof-of-Stake (PoS) testnet designed to simulate the behavior of Ethereum and Alchemy [3] as it offers a powerful blockchain or web3 development platform.

6 Data Model and Protocol Flow

In this section, we present the data model (Sect. 6.1) and different use-cases along with their respective protocol flow (Sect. 6.2).

6.1 Data Model

To begin, Table 1 outlines the mathematical notations utilized in various protocol flows, and these notations are self-explanatory.

Table 1. Cryptographic Notations

Notations	Description
$User$	User of the system(Client interface).
$NIDVS$	A third party verification server who verifies the authenticity of NID.
PVS	Property Verification Server.
K_U	Public key of the sender.
K_U^{-1}	Private key of the sender
$sign(D)$	Signing data D using user's private key; $\{D\}_{K_U^{-1}}$.
N_i	A fresh nonce.
$\{\}_k$	Encryption operation using a public key K.
$H_{sha}(M)$	SHA-256 hashing operation of message M.
$H_{keccak}(M)$	Keccak256 hashing operation of message M.
$[...]_{https}$	Communication over HTTPS channel.

The system utilizes a request-response protocol in which a request is submitted and a respective response is returned. There are different requests and responses utilized in the system. Table 2 presents the data model to denote what each request and response consists of. There are seven requests (*req*) such as *reqRegistration, reqNIDVerification, reqTokenCreation, reqVerifyProperty, reqTokenUpdate, reqTokenAddress* and *reqReadyTokenData.* Their respective responses (*resp*) are *respRegistration, respNIDVerification, respTokenCreation, respVerifyProperty, respTokenUpdate, respTokenAddress* and , *respReadyTokenData* respectively. There are other data as well such as *userInfo* which holds the data related to a user. The *propertyData* includes data representing a property. When we tokenize a property, the system utilizes *propertyData*, $tokenID$, *agreementDate*, and $renterID$ (if appropriate). All of these data are available within *textualTokenData*. The *updateTokenData* is used while executing actions such as buy, sell, rent, leave token and the system takes *newAgreementDate, newOwnerUserID* or *newRenterUserID.* Other data are self-explanatory and hence, their discussion is excluded for brevity.

Algorithm: Next, we present the algorithm encoding three important functions in Algorithm 1. These functions present the pseudocode for user registration, token creation and token usage illustrating the buying, selling, renting, and leave action of a property. The REGISTRATION function is used to register a new user in the system. The function first extracts $userInfo, userID$ and

Table 2. Data Model

req = {*reqRegistration, reqNIDVerification, reqTokenCreation, reqVerifyProperty, reqTokenUpdate, reqTokenAddress, reqReadyTokenData* }
resp = {*respRegistration, respNIDVerification, respTokenCreation, respVerifyProperty, respTokenUpdate, respTokenAddress, respReadyTokenData* }
reqRegistration = { *registrationData* }
reqNIDVerification = { *NID* }
reqTokenCreation = { *propertyData* }
reqVerifyProperty = { propertyData }
reqTokenUpdate = { tokenID, newOwnerUserID $\parallel$ newRenterUserID, newAgreementDate, actionType }
reqTokenAddress = { request address of a ready token by *tokenID* }
reqReadyTokenData = { $dataAddr_{readyToken}$ }
respRegistration = { Registration Successful message }
respNIDVerification = { return verification status in boolean }
respTokenCreation = { Successful token creation message }
respVerifyProperty = { return verification status in boolean }
respTokenUpdate = { return update status in boolean }
respTokenAddress = { $dataAddr_{readyToken}$ }
respReadyTokenData = { *textualTokenData*, *propertyImage* }
userInfo = {userID, Name, DoB, NID Number, Present Address, Permanent Address, Phone Number}
propertyData = { propertyAddress, propertyImage, propertyRentPrice/propertySellPrice, userID, status }
registrationData = { *userInfo, userID, password* }
userID = { K_U }
textualTokenData = { propertyData (except *propertyImage*), agreementDate, renterID }
updatedTokenData = { hash of *propertyImage*, and *textualTokenData* where agreementDate=newAgreementDate, userID=newOwnerUserID $\parallel$ renterID=newRenterUserID }
$hashedCred = H_{keccak}(password, userID)$
$dataAddr_X$ = { data address X in IPFS }

password from *registrationData*. Next, the *reqVerifyNID* function is invoked, which verifies the *userInfo* and returns a Boolean response. IF the response is not *true*, the function rejects the registration call. Otherwise, *userInfo* is stored in IPFS that returns a hashed address (*publicDataHash*) of the contents. Meanwhile, *userID* and *password* are hashed using the *Keccak*256 algorithm. Finally, *publicDataHash* and the hashed data are stored in the blockchain.

Algorithm 1. Property Tokenization

```
...
function Registration(reqistrationData)
    Extract userInfo, userID and password from registrationData
    isVerified := reqVerifyNID(userInfo)
    if isVerified != true then return reject registration;
    else
        publicDataHash := storeIPFS(userInfo)
        hashedCred := H_keccak(userID, password)
        actionStatus := storeInBlockchain(publicDataHash, hashedCred)
        return respRegistration
function TokenCreation(propertyData)
    Extract propertyImage from propertyData;
    Extract the rest textualData from propertyData;
    isVerified := reqVerifyProperty(propertyData)
    if isVerified != true then return reject token creation;
    else
        hashedImgAddress := storeInIPFS(propertyImage)
        propertyAllDataHash := storeInIPFS(textualData, hashedImgAddress)
        actionStatus := storeInBlockchain(propertyAllDataHash)
        return respTokenCreation
function TokenUpdate(tokenID, newUserID, newAgreementDate, actionType)
    tokenDataAddress := reqTokenAddress(tokenID)
    readyTokenData := reqReadyTokenData(tokenDataAddress)
    updatedTokenData := updateTokenData( readyTokenData, newUserID,newAgreement
  Date, actionType )
    hashedUpdatedTokenDataAddr := storeInIPFS(updatedTokenData)
    actionStatus = storeInBlockchain(hashedUpdatedTokenDataAddr)
    return respRegistration
...
```

The *TokenCreation* function is responsible to create a token for adding a new property to the system. The function first extracts *propertyImage* and the rest of the *textualData*. Next, *reqVerifyProperty* checks the authenticity of the property data, and if fake, the request is rejected. Otherwise, *propertyImage* and *textualData* are stored in IPFS. Finally, hashed addresses of all data are stored in blockchain and the function returns a success response.

The *TokenUpdate* function is responsible for buying, selling, renting and leave actions. All of these actions require *userID* (for selling, buying) or *renterID* and *agreementData* (for renting and leaving). The function first fetches the *hashedAddress* of a token from Blockchain using *tokenID*, and next, the respective token data is fetched from IPFS. Consequently, *updateTokenData* action is invoked that updates token data. The *actionType* field consists one of "buy", "sell", "rent" or "leave" string and execute the respective task. Finally, the updated data are stored in IPFS and the returned hashed address is stored in the blockchain mapped with the old tokenID.

6.2 Protocol Flow

Now, we present different use-cases and their respective protocol flows involving various components of our system. We cover three use-cases: i) User registration and login, ii) Property token creation and iii) Buying, selling, renting or leaving a token. These use-cases are discussed next.

User registration & Login: In the proposed system, a new user must register in order to interact with our DApp. The protocol flow of this process is provided in Table 3 and discussed next.

Table 3. Registration protocol

M_0	$User \rightarrow DApp : [N1, reqRegistration, sign(registrationData)]_{https}$	
M_1	$DApp \rightarrow NIDVS :$	$[N2, reqNIDVerification\ ]_{https}$
M_2	$NIDVS \rightarrow DApp :$	$[N2,\ respNIDVerification]_{https}$
M_3	$DApp \rightarrow IPFS :$	$[N3, userInfo]_{https}$
M_4	$IPFS \rightarrow DApp :$	$[N3, H_{sha}(dataAddr_{userInfo})]_{https}$
M_5	$DApp \rightarrow Blockchain :$	$[N4, H_{sha}(dataAddr_{userInfo}), hashedCred]_{https}$
M_6	$Blockchain \rightarrow Dapp :$	$[N4, TRUE]_{https}$
M_7	$DApp \rightarrow User :$	$[N1, respRegistration]_{https}$

i The user sends a registration request *reqRegistration* through a registration form to DApp. A signature of the sent data is also passed within the request body (M0 in Table 3).

ii The DApp extracts different identity data and birth date through *reqNID-Verification* call to *NIDVS* to verify the user (M1 in Table 3).

iii *NIDVS* replies with a boolean response $respNIDVerification$ (M2 in Table 3).

iv Next, the $userInfo$ is sent to IPFS blockchain platform to store the data (M3 in Table 3). After storing the data, IPFS returns the hashed location of user data $dataAddr_{userInfo}$ back to the DApp (M4 in Table 3).

v Next, the DApp sends the hashed address, *userID* and *hashedCred* in the blockchain (M5 in Table 3).

vi Finally, after storing the data successfully, the DApp receives a response with a status TRUE (M6 in Table 3) and consequently, DApp displays a confirmation message from *respRegistration* (M7 in Table 3).

The subsequent use-cases require each user to log in to the system to access services. Similarly to the registration protocol, the login protocol requires the user to provide their userID (Wallet address) and password through their browser. The underlying algorithm executes the $H_{keccak}(userID, password)$

operation and matches the stored *hashedCred* given by the user during registration. If matched, the user logs in the system.

Property Token Creation: Now, we discuss how an individual token is created against a property so that it becomes available in the marketplace. The screenshot of the page is provided in Fig. 3 and the flow is presented in Table 4. Next we elaborate the protocol flow.

Table 4. Token Creation/Add property protocol

M_0	$User \rightarrow DApp:$	$[N1, reqTokenCreation, sign(propertyData)\ ]_{https}$
M_1	$DApp \rightarrow PVS:$	$[N2, reqVerifyProperty\ ]_{https}$
M_2	$PVS \rightarrow DApp:$	$[N2, respVerifyProperty]_{https}$
M_3	$DApp \rightarrow IPFS:$	$[N3, propertyImage]_{https}$
M_4	$IPFS \rightarrow DApp:$	$[N3, H_{sha}(dataAddr_{propertyImage})]_{https}$
M_5	$DApp \rightarrow IPFS:$	$[N4, textualTokenData, H_{sha}(dataAddr_{propertyImage})]_{https}$
M_6	$IPFS \rightarrow DApp:$	$[N4, H_{sha}(dataAddr_{readyToken})]_{https}$
M_7	$DApp \rightarrow Blockchain:$	$[N5, H_{sha}(dataAddr_{readyToken})]_{https}$
M_8	$Blockchain \rightarrow DApp:$	$[N5, TRUE]_{https}$
M_9	$DApp \rightarrow User:$	$[N1, respTokenCreation\ ]_{https}$

i The owner submits a token creation request $reqTokenCreation$ attached with a digital sign to the DApp (M0 in Table 4).

ii Next, the DApp extracts and sends the $propertyData$ to the property verification server PVS (M1 in Table 4). If verified, the PVS replies back with a Boolean status $respVerifyProperty$ (M2 in Table 4). The property is eligible now to get a unique $tokenID$.

iii To store the property information, DApp sends all data of the property to the IPFS database in two consequent steps. First, DApp sends $propertyImage$ (M3 in Table 4) and IPFS replies with an image address (M4 in Table 4). Next, the DApp sends $textualTokenData$ along with the returned hashed address of the image to IPFS (M5 in Table 4) and this time, IPFS returns another hashed address (M6 in Table 4). The token data is now ready to get stored in blockchain.

iv At this point, the DApp sends a token creation call to the blockchain (M7 in Table 4) with the hash value $H_{sha}(dataAddr_{propertyData})$ received in step M6. Getting this, the underlying algorithm generates a random unique number as a token against the particular property as well as checks if it is available for a new token or not. If the number is available, it is registered as the $tokenID$ of the property. Then, the $tokenID$ along with the hashed value returned from IPFS is stored in the blockchain and in future the hashed address of the token can be mapped through this $tokenID$ within the blockchain.

v Finally, a TRUE status is sent from blockchain to DApp, denoting a successful token creation and the DApp shows a confirmation message (M8 and M9 in Table 4).

Buying, Selling, Renting or Leaving Token: Now, we explore the third use-case. It is to be noted that these four operations are different, however, the protocol remains same. The protocol is presented in Table 5 and is discussed next.

Table 5. Buy/Sell/Rent/Leave protocol

M_0	$User \rightarrow DApp:$	$[N1, reqTokenUpdate, sign(tokenID)]_{https}$
M_1	$DApp \rightarrow Blockchain:$	$[N1, \{reqTokenAddress\}]_{https}$
M_2	$Blockchain \rightarrow DApp:$	$[N1, respTokenAddress]_{https}$
M_3	$DApp \rightarrow IPFS:$	$[N1, reqReadyTokenData]_{https}$
M_4	$IPFS \rightarrow DApp:$	$[N1, respReadyTokenData]_{https}$
M_5	$DApp \rightarrow IPFS:$	$[N1, updatedTokenData]_{https}$
M_6	$IPFS \rightarrow DApp:$	$[N1, H_{sha}(dataAddr_{updatedTokenData})]_{https}$
M_7	$DApp \rightarrow Blockchain:$	$[N2, H_{sha}(dataAddr_{updatedTokenData})]_{https}$
M_8	$Blockchain \rightarrow DApp:$	$[N2, TRUE]_{https}$
M_9	$DApp \rightarrow User:$	$[N1, respTokenUpdate]_{https}$

i To buy/sell/rent/leave a property, the user submits a form from webpage (Fig. 3b) which initiates the *reqTokenUpdate* request. The *reqTokenUpdate* includes *tokenID*, *actionType* such as "buy", "sell", "rent", "leave" and the updated value (M0 in Table 5). The DApp extracts the *tokenID* and requests the token address from the blockchain (M1 in Table 5)

ii If available, the hash address of that particular token data is returned to DApp and DApp queries IPFS to return the respective data, and upon request, IPFS returns *textualTokenData* and *propertyImage* via the *respReadyTokenData* response to DApp(M2, M3 and M4 in Table 5).

iii Next, if being rented, the DApp updates the *renterID* and *agreementData* of the property. If being purchased by a new owner, the *userID* of the *propertyData* is updated. Next, the new data is stored in IPFS and the price of selling or renting a property is transferred from consumer's wallet to owner's wallet (M5 in Table 5).

iv IPFS returns a new hash address of the updated data, which is then stored in the blockchain (M6 and M7 in Table 5).

v Finally, the blockchain returns a TRUE status to DApp and the DApp sends a confirmation message through *respTokenUpdate* response (M8 and M9 in Table 5).

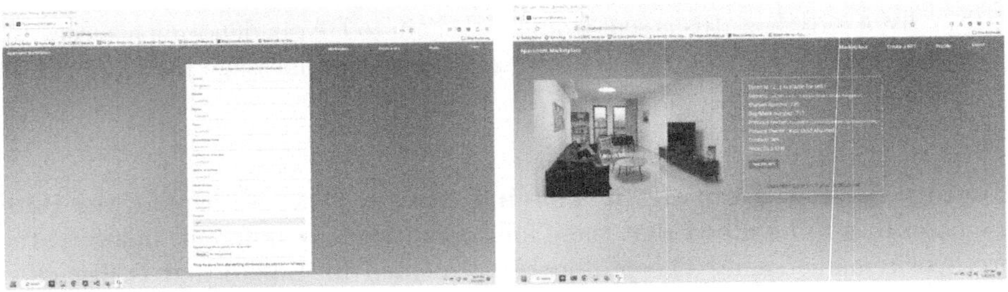

(a) Token Creation (b) Buy/Sell/Rent/Leave Token Page

Fig. 3. Create, Buy, Sell, Rent and Leave a Token

7 Analysis and Discussion

In this section, we analyze the formulated requirements (Sect. 7.1), calculate the cost associated with different use cases (Sect. 7.2), and discuss the advantages (Sect. 7.4), limitations and future direction of our research (Sect. 7.5).

7.1 Analyzing Requirements

Functional Requirements: In the proposed system, users are registered after successful NID verification ensuring *FR2*. Once registered, owners can easily create tokens to buy/sell properties, whereas renters can rent rooms and flats through these tokens easily ensuring the fulfillment of *FR1* and *FR5*. The system is coupled with decentralized systems such as IPFS and Blockchain where no single entity can control the system and each token-related activity generates a blockchain transaction recorded on the blockchain in a transparent way, thereby ensuring *FR3* and *FR6*. The execution of each transaction is validated through a node connected in a peer-to-peer network, and the IPFS also works on a peer-to-peer protocol that satisfies *FR4*.

Security Requirements: This system is designed with NID verification and log in mechanism to guarantee the identity of its users and hence, it satisfies *SR1*. Hashes of the data stored in the IPFS are stored in the blockchain which ensures the data integrity and satisfies *SR2*. The use of digital signature fulfills *SR3*. All data are transmitted through the encrypted HTTPS channels to ensure *SR4*. Additionally, the use of nonce ensures the prevention of reply attacks, satisfying SR6. Finally, The system requires gas (fee) to execute different actions and the cost is paid by the user. Therefore, *SR5* is unlikely to happen as this attack would cost the attacker a lot of fees which would not be beneficial for the attacker.

7.2 Cost Analysis

All interface deployment and transaction expenses are shown in Table 6. Since the price of cryptocurrency is volatile, we are presenting the cost as per August 9, 2023.

From Table 6, it is evident that the cost of smart contract deployment is the highest among all categories. However, this should not be problematic as the contract is deployed only once when the system is initiated for the first time, and thus charged once. Additionally, this payment is not paid by the users, rather it is paid by the authority which owns the system. The rest of the actions consume a relatively low amount of gas (fee). In addition, the gas cost for renting is only about 0.43 USD, which is a user-friendly cost scheme.

Table 6. Cost Analysis

Category	Gas Cost (ETH)	Dollar (USD)	BDT(TAKA)
Contract Deploy	0.0597	159.88	18806.32
Registration	0.000235417999998976	0.63	74.11
Token Creation	0.000435874000011264	1.17	137.62
Buy Token	0.00022198	0.59	69.40
Sell Token	0.000416236000002048	1.11	130.57
Rent Token	0.000162284	0.43	50.58
Return Token	0.000123609999998976	0.33	38.82

7.3 Feature Comparison with Existing Platforms

The comparison presented in Table 7 shows that existing blockchain real estate platforms have varying features for fractional ownership, renting, and token utilization. Propy offers fractional ownership using an ERC-20 based token but lacks rental functionality, while Harbor is limited to commercial properties without any token support. RealIT and Atlant both offer fractional ownership and renting and each of them uses their own ERC-20 based tokens on Ethereum. In contrast, our system uniquely leverages an ERC-721 token, which supports both fractional ownership and renting. This differentiates it with existing systems, providing unique asset representation compared to the more generic ERC-20 tokens used by other platforms.

7.4 Advantages

This system offers many advantages. In the following, we are going to highlight some of them:

- Users have the freedom to buy/sell/rent a flat or even an individual room as per their needs.
- The system uses NID verification of the users and providing unique token ids to each individual property to reduce fraudulence in the system.

Table 7. Features of existing platforms

Existing System	Fractional ownership (rooms)	Renting	Token	Blockchain Platform
Propy [12]	Yes	No	PRO Token (ERC-20)	Ethereum
Harbor [9]	No	No	No	Ethereum
RealIT [15]	Yes	Yes	RealToken (ERC-20)	Ethereum
Atlant [1]	Yes	Yes	ATL Token (ERC-20)	Ethereum
Our System	Yes	Yes	ERC-721	Ethereum

- We are assuring peer to peer transactions to avoid any unwanted incident due to the involvement of third party brokers in this field.
- If a property is occupied, it does not appear in the system therefore, any fraudulent attempt to sell or to fake vacancy is not possible.

7.5 Limitations and Future Works

In many countries, e.g. Bangladesh, cryptocurrencies and cryptotransactions are not fully legalized. Therefore, it might be difficult to implement such a system in those countries. Moreover, the unstable gas price of Ethereum may create concerns for the users; therefore, in the future we will explore how a consortium blockchain can be used to stabilize or eliminate the gas cost completely. Additionally, we will assess the performance of the system to analyze the probable behavior in large-scale deployment scenarios.

8 Conclusion

In this research, we have presented a solution through which users can buy, sell and rent their properties by leveraging blockchain, IPFS and tokenization. The aim of this work is to eliminate existing fraud, improve security and reduce user complexities of traditional systems. We have presented the architecture based on a well-established threat model and different functional and security requirements. We have detailed the protocol flows of different use-cases and have verified the feasibility of implementation and explored the associated user cost. We believe that such a system can definitely help users address multiple challenges faced in the current setting.

References

1. ATLANT World's Real Estate Blockchain Platform (Mar 2022). https://atlant.io, [Online; accessed 5. Oct. 2024]
2. Online Home Rental Market (Mar 2023). https://www.futuremarketinsights.com/reports/online-home-rental-market. Accessed 2 Oct 2024
3. Alchemy - the web3 development platform (Aug 2024). https://www.alchemy.com. Accessed 10 Aug 2024
4. Asset Tokenization: Basics, Benefits & Blockchain | Chainlink (Aug 2024). https://chain.link/education/asset-tokenization#how-does-asset-tokenization-work. Accessed 11 Aug 2024
5. Dubai Land Department Real Estate Blockchain: International Telecommunication Union. https://www.itu.int/net4/wsis/archive/stocktaking/Project/Details?projectId=1515496900. Accessed 11 Aug 2024
6. Ethereum development documentation | ethereum.org (Aug 2024). https://ethereum.org/en/developers/docs. Accessed 8 Aug 2024
7. Ethereum Improvement Proposals (Aug 2024). https://eips.ethereum.org/EIPS/eip-721. Accessed 10 Aug 2024
8. Fungible vs non-fungible tokens: What's the difference? (Aug 2024). https://www.moonpay.com/learn/blockchain/fungible-vs-non-fungible-tokens. Accessed 11 Aug 2024
9. Harbor Custom Homes (Oct 2024). https://harborcustomhomescrypto.com. Accessed 5 Oct 2024
10. Hardhat | Ethereum development environment for professionals by Nomic Foundation (Aug 2024). https://hardhat.org. Accessed 10 Aug 2024
11. Node.js — Run JavaScript Everywhere (Aug 2024). https://nodejs.org/en. Accessed 8 Aug 2024
12. Propy | 24/7 Real Estate Closings Powered by Tech (Sep 2024). https://propy.com/home. Accessed 5 Oct 2024
13. React (Aug 2024). https://react.dev. Accessed 10 Aug 2024
14. Real Estate Rental Market Growth Revenue, Industry Analysis, Overview By 2033 (Jan 2024). https://www.thebusinessresearchcompany.com/report/real-estate-rental-global-market-report. Accessed 2 Oct 2024
15. RealT, Inc. (May 2024). https://realt.co. Accessed 5 Oct 2024
16. Rental Listing Scams (Feb 2024). https://consumer.ftc.gov/articles/rental-listing-scams. Accessed 31 July 2024
17. Solana Documentation | Solana (Aug 2024). https://solana.com/docs. Accessed 11 Aug 2024
18. Tailwind CSS - Rapidly build modern websites without ever leaving your HTML. (Aug 2024). https://tailwindcss.com. Accessed 10 Aug 2024
19. Welcome to Cardano Docs | Cardano Docs (Aug 2024). https://docs.cardano.org. Accessed 11 Aug 2024
20. What is asset tokenization? | Hedera (Aug 2024). https://hedera.com/learning/tokens/what-is-asset-tokenization. Accessed 11 Aug 2024
21. What is IPFS? | IPFS Docs (Aug 2024). https://docs.ipfs.tech/concepts/what-is-ipfs. Accessed 11 Aug 2024

22. Ann O'Connell, A.c.U.B.S.o.L.: Can Our Landlord Evict Us to Move the Landlord's Family Member In? Www.nolo (Apr 2024). https://www.nolo.com/legal-encyclopedia/question-evict-landlord-family-member-28362.html
23. Association, N.A.: Apartment Rental Application Fraud Omnipresent, Increasing | National Apartment Association (Jan 2024). https://www.naahq.org/apartment-rental-application-fraud-omnipresent-increasing. Accessed 31 July 2024
24. Azibo: Can You Pay Rent in Cash? What Renters Need to Know - Azibo (Feb 2024). https://www.azibo.com/blog/can-you-pay-rent-in-cash. Accessed 1 Aug 2024
25. Cahyani, A.M., Nuraina, E., Styaningrum, F.: Fraudulent financial reporting on property, real estate, and building construction companies. Assets: Jurnal Akuntansi dan Pendidikan **10**(2), 132–146 (2021)
26. Chavez-Dreyfuss, G.: Sweden tests blockchain technology for land registry. Reuters (Jun 2016). https://www.reuters.com/article/us-sweden-blockchain/sweden-tests-blockchain-technology-for-land-registry-idUSKCN0Z22KV
27. Chowdhury, M.J.M., et al.: A comparative analysis of distributed ledger technology platforms. IEEE Access **7**(1), 167930–167943 (2019)
28. Falcon, J.: Fraudulent rental applications have spiked during pandemic - HousingWire. HousingWire (May 2020). https://www.housingwire.com/articles/fraudulent-rental-applications-have-spiked-during-pandemic
29. Garcia-Teruel, R.M.: Legal challenges and opportunities of blockchain technology in the real estate sector. J. Property, Plann. Environment. Law **12**(2), 129–145 (2020)
30. Gupta, A., Rathod, J., Patel, D., Bothra, J., Shanbhag, S., Bhalerao, T.: Tokenization of real estate using blockchain technology. In: Zhou, J., et al. (eds.) ACNS 2020. LNCS, vol. 12418, pp. 77–90. Springer, Cham (2020). https://doi.org/10.1007/978-3-030-61638-0_5
31. Innago: The Risks of Accepting Cash Payments for Rent - Innago. Innago (Mar 20119). https://innago.com/risks-cash-payments
32. Joshi, S., Choudhury, A.: Tokenization of real estate assets using blockchain. Int. J. Intell. Inform. Technol. (IJIIT) **18**(3), 1–12 (2022)
33. Kabir, S.F.: Seeking Shelter In The Big City - Issues Between Landlord and Tenant In Bangladesh (Oct 2008). https://www.vertexchambers.com/blawg-list/seeking-shelter-in-the-big-city-issues-between-landlord-and-tenant-in-bangladesh-october-2012-issue-1. Accessed 4 Aug 2024
34. Konashevych, O.: Constraints and benefits of the blockchain use for real estate and property rights. J. Property, Plann. Environment. Law **12**(2), 109–127 (2020)
35. Mottaghi, S.F., Steininger, B.I., Yanagawa, N.: Real estate insights: The current state and the new future of tokenization in real estate. J. Property Invest. Fin. (2024)
36. Nandi, M., Bhattacharjee, R.K., Jha, A., Barbhuiya, F.A.: A secured land registration framework on blockchain. In: ISEA-ISAP, pp. 130–138. IEEE (2020)
37. Reporter, G.s.: Hidden landlords: renters' woes soar as property owners hide their identities. the Guardian (Jan 2024). https://www.theguardian.com/us-news/2023/nov/16/hidden-landlords-limited-liability-companies-llcs-rental-property
38. Sharma, A., Sharma, A., Tripathi, A., Chaudhary, A.: Real estate registry platform through nft tokenization using blockchain. In: ICDT, pp. 335–340 (2024)
39. Sheldon, M.D.: Tracking tangible asset ownership and provenance with blockchain. J. Inf. Syst. **36**(3), 153–175 (2022)
40. Shostack, A.: Threat modeling: Designing for security. John Wiley & Sons (2014)

41. Spielman, A.: Blockchain: digitally rebuilding the real estate industry. Ph.D. thesis, Massachusetts Institute of Technology (2016)
42. Thosar, A., Hame, M., Sarode, A., Kaur, P.: Land registry management using blockachain. In: ICSIDEMPC, pp. 335–340 (2020)
43. Weingärtner, T.: Tokenization of physical assets and the impact of Iot and AI. In: European Union Blockchain Observatory and Forum. vol. 10, pp. 1–16 (2019)
44. Zhang, L., Ci, L., Wu, Y., Wiwatanapataphee, B.: The real estate time-stamping and registration system based on ethereum blockchain. Blockchain: Res. Appl. **5**(1), 100175 (2024)

Bitcoin Halving Events: Historical Analysis and Strategic Insights for Miners

Daewoong Cho[1(✉)], Gowri Ramachandran[1], Raja Jurdak[1], and Salil S. Kanhere[2]

[1] School of Computer Science, Queensland University of Technology, Brisbane, QLD, Australia
daewoong.cho@hdr.qut.edu.au, {g.ramachandran,r.jurdak}@qut.edu.au

[2] School of Computer Science and Engineering, The University of New South Wales, Sydney, NSW, Australia
salil.kanhere@unsw.edu.au

Abstract. Completing the fourth Bitcoin halving event in April 2024 has introduced new complexities to the Bitcoin mining landscape, underscoring the necessity for reevaluating blockchain sustainability. As mining rewards diminish, sustaining effective incentives for miners becomes increasingly critical. This study conducts a rigorous analysis of halving dynamics, leveraging historical data from previous halving events to elucidate the intricate relationships between mining rewards, cryptocurrency prices, and operational costs. Our findings provide strategic insights into how these factors influence mining profitability, offering miners essential guidance for adapting to the evolving challenges of the halving environment. By dissecting the impact of reward reductions on mining operations, this research not only enhances understanding of the drivers of profitability but also equips miners with the knowledge required to maintain robust operations. This study contributes significantly to the broader discourse on blockchain resilience, offering actionable insights for sustaining a robust and adaptive Bitcoin ecosystem.

Keywords: Blockchain · Cryptocurrency · Mining Profitability · Halving Events · Sustainable Mining

1 Introduction

The exponential growth of blockchain technology has significantly heightened academic interest in unraveling the complexities of blockchain mining profitability. As the cornerstone of decentralized systems, mining plays a crucial role in ensuring transactional security and maintaining the immutable integrity of the blockchain. Despite its paramount importance, the cost-effectiveness of mining operations and the multifaceted factors influencing profitability remain subjects of immense scholarly significance and ongoing research. The dynamic interplay between technological advancements, operational efficiency, and market fluctuations drives academic curiosity and excitement, pushing efforts to decode the

S. Kanhere et al. (Eds.): SDLT 2024, CCIS 2453, pp. 38–54, 2025.
https://doi.org/10.1007/978-981-96-4442-1_3

economic viability of blockchain mining and its broader implications for the future of the digital economy.

Within the Bitcoin blockchain ecosystem, mining occupies a pivotal role, facilitating both the operation and security of the entire network. Miners, the key actors in this process, engage in the competitive and complex task of solving intricate mathematical puzzles through the Proof of Work mechanism to validate and create new blocks [1].

In return for their efforts, miners gain the privilege of creating new blocks and receiving a certain amount of newly minted Bitcoins. However, this process is fraught with complexities. With each halving event, mining rewards are reduced, gradually decreasing the total supply of newly created Bitcoins. The fourth Bitcoin subsidy halving event, which has already occurred, is a crucial milestone in the ongoing development of the Bitcoin ecosystem. Existing research [2,3] on Bitcoin halving events has primarily focused on retrospective analysis, with less emphasis on predicting and preparing for such events.

In return for their efforts, miners gain the privilege of creating new blocks and receiving a certain amount of newly minted Bitcoins. However, this process is fraught with complexities. With each halving event, mining rewards are reduced, leading to a gradual decrease in the total supply of newly created Bitcoins. The fourth Bitcoin subsidy halving event, which has already occurred, stands as a crucial milestone in the ongoing development of the Bitcoin ecosystem. Existing research [2,3] on Bitcoin halving events has primarily focused on retrospective analysis, with less emphasis on predicting and preparing for such events.

In light of the completed 2024 Bitcoin halving event, which reduced block rewards from 6.25 BTC to 3.125 BTC, miners face the challenge of sustaining their revenue levels. To address this, our research provides a quantitative analysis of the impact of this halving event is based on historical data, offering data-driven recommendations for miners to navigate the evolving Bitcoin mining landscape.

Our research contributions are summarised into two key aspects:

- Comprehensive Historical Analysis: The study offers a detailed historical analysis of Bitcoin halving events, exploring key metrics and uncovering insights into Bitcoin's transactional, economic, and market behaviors.
- Strategic Considerations for Miners: The study provides guidance on how miners can adapt to reduced subsidies and increased competition, emphasizing efficiency, elastic mining models, and sustainability. It equips miners with valuable information to optimize operations, address environmental concerns, and sustain profitability amidst changing industry dynamics.

The subsequent sections of this paper are organised as follows. In Sect. 2, an in-depth exploration of blockchain technology and the Bitcoin halving event is provided. Section 3 reviews the existing literature related to past halving events. Section 4 focuses on the data analysis of historical halving events, investigating the relationship between cryptocurrency prices and reward reductions. Subsequently, Sect. 5 delves into observations regarding the completed halving event, based on the data analysis in the previous section. This information is then used to analyse profitability, leading to a discussion of the findings. Finally, Sect. 6 summarises the outcomes and outlines potential directions for future research.

2 Background

This section provides an overview of the blockchain and mining, followed by an explanation of the Bitcoin halving mechanism and its significance in controlling coin supply and inflation.

Fig. 1. An overview of the Bitcoin mining process, illustrating the key steps involved in validating transactions and securing the blockchain

2.1 Blockchain and Mining

Blockchain is a foundational technology underlying cryptocurrencies and various decentralised applications. It functions as a distributed, immutable ledger that records transactions across a network of interconnected nodes. Each transaction is grouped into a block cryptographically linked to the previous block, forming a chain of blocks, hence the term "blockchain". This structure ensures transparency, security, and tamper resistance, making it vital in revolutionizing digital transactions and data management across industries [1].

Figure 1 illustrates the fundamental process of blockchain mining in the operation and maintenance of the blockchain network. Miners with powerful computational resources compete to solve complex mathematical puzzles through the Proof of Work consensus mechanism. The first miner to solve the puzzle successfully earns the right to validate and append the block of transactions to the blockchain. As a reward for their efforts and resources expended, miners are granted new coins, known as block rewards, which constitute the primary source of newly minted cryptocurrencies. It also plays an essential role in issuing new cryptocurrency units through mechanisms like proof-of-work. Mining's energy-intensive nature has sparked discussions on environmental sustainability and alternative consensus mechanisms [4].

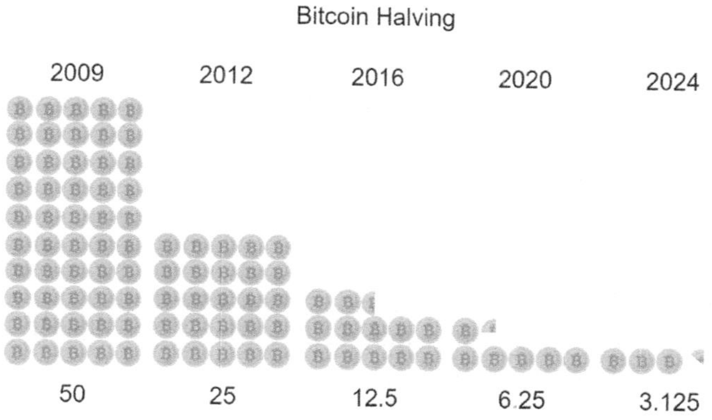

Fig. 2. A depiction of the Bitcoin halving event, which occurs approximately every four years, reducing the block reward by half. This mechanism plays a crucial role in controlling Bitcoin's supply and influencing market dynamics

2.2 Transaction Fees

Bitcoin transaction fees are vital for the cryptocurrency ecosystem, incentivising miners and ensuring network security. Users can add fees to expedite transactions, with higher fees leading to quicker confirmations and lower fees potentially causing delays during network congestion [5,6]. Factors like transaction size and network demand influence fees, creating competition among users. Those offering higher fees experience faster transaction processing, particularly when demand for block space is high [7].

2.3 The Significance of Halving Events

The Bitcoin halving mechanism is an essential and inherent feature of the protocol, designed to control coin supply and inflation over time. Approximately every four years, or after 210,000 blocks, the mining reward is halved as described in Fig. 2. This event, known as the halving, reduces the rate at which new Bitcoins are created, contributing to a controlled and predictable issuance schedule.

The occurrence of halving events has a profound impact on the dynamics of the Bitcoin ecosystem, particularly concerning mining incentives. Some might speculate that miner incentives would diminish as mining rewards decrease during halving events. However, historical data from previous halvings reveals a fascinating paradox. Despite the reduction in rewards, the price of Bitcoin has historically tended to increase following halving events [8]. This price appreciation not only offsets the reduction in block rewards but also enhances mining incentives, effectively encouraging miners to continue their operations and support the network.

Understanding this interplay between mining rewards, cryptocurrency price, and miner incentives is crucial in assessing the sustainability and longevity of the Bitcoin network. By delving into historical data and analyzing the complexities surrounding halving events, this paper aims to provide valuable insights into the mechanisms that drive mining incentives and their implications for the broader cryptocurrency ecosystem.

3 Related Work

To contextualise our research, we review existing literature on previous halving events and their implications for mining incentives. We identify gaps in the research landscape that our study aims to address.

Meynkhard [2] reviewed existing literature on previous halving events and their implications for mining incentives, identifying research gaps. It built upon prior studies by investigating the fair market value of Bitcoin and its correlation with halving events, using econometric models and time series analysis to understand price dynamics. Addressing the lack of specific research on Bitcoin's fair market value during halving events, the study shed light on the influence of halving events on Bitcoin's price fluctuations, considering other market dynamics. Furthermore, it explored additional factors affecting Bitcoin's valuation and employed predictive modeling to forecast the consequences of future halving events, providing valuable insights for investors, researchers, and policymakers in anticipating market behavior following such events. In summary, the paper contributed to the field by focusing on the impact of halving events on Bitcoin's fair market value and using rigorous methodologies to understand its price behavior.

Kroll et al. [9] utilised predictive modeling to forecast the future trends of Bitcoin mining activity. By analyzing historical data and considering factors such as changes in block rewards and mining difficulty, the researchers developed predictive models to anticipate the potential impact on the Bitcoin mining ecosystem. These models aimed to project how mining activity might have evolved in response to varying market conditions and technological advancements. Through the predictive modeling approach, the paper sought to provide insights into potential scenarios related to Bitcoin mining. This allowed researchers and stakeholders to understand better how the mining landscape could have unfolded, thus informing strategic decision-making and policy considerations in the rapidly evolving cryptocurrency ecosystem.

Wang et al. [10] focused on measuring and analyzing the Bitcoin network from the perspective of mining pools. The paper specifically examined the activities of mining pools in the Bitcoin network. Mining pools involve multiple miners collaborating to generate blocks and distribute rewards. This paper places particular emphasis on studying the operations of these mining pools. In particular, the paper investigated the changes in mining activities concerning Bitcoin's halving events. Halving events involved reducing the block rewards for miners, which could impact their earnings and mining difficulty. The study analysed the effects of these halving events on mining pool activities and the network as a whole, exploring block creation frequency, changes in mining participation, and other relevant factors. By approaching Bitcoin's network measurement and analysis from the perspective of mining pools, the paper aimed to provide valuable insights into Bitcoin's mining activities. Through the examination of mining pool behaviors and network dynamics, it contributed to evaluating and understanding the robustness and decentralization of the Bitcoin ecosystem.

Fantazzini et al. [11] investigated the impact of Bitcoin's mining hashrate on its price. The study analysed how the hashrate, representing the computational work in mining, influenced the cryptocurrency's value, emphasizing its significance for network security and mining profitability. Utilizing statistical methods and time series analysis, the research explored the correlation between hashrate and Bitcoin's price fluctuations to understand their interplay. The study found that the hashrate had a positive impact on Bitcoin's price, indicating that an increase in mining hashrate corresponded to higher cryptocurrency valuations. However, the relationship between hashrate and price was not found to be linear, suggesting that other factors also influence Bitcoin's price dynamics.

Jireh et al. [3] investigated the price volatility trends of Bitcoin from the perspective of its halving events. The paper focused on the price volatility during the halving cycles of Bitcoin. Halving events occurred when the block rewards for Bitcoin miners were reduced, and the study explored the impact of these events on Bitcoin's price. The paper utilised the MSGARCH (Multivariate Singular Spectrum Generalised Autoregressive Conditional Heteroskedasticity) model to analyse Bitcoin's price volatility. By employing the MSGARCH model, the paper aimed to examine the volatility patterns of Bitcoin during its halving cycles and investigate how these events influenced the price volatility of Bitcoin. The study sought to provide valuable insights into the effect of halving events on the price fluctuations of Bitcoin.

While previous research [2,3,9–13] has extensively analyzed the historical impact of Bitcoin halving events on mining incentives, few studies provide proactive strategies for miners to navigate future halvings. This study fills this gap by offering both a comprehensive historical analysis and forward-looking insights aimed at sustaining miner profitability.

4 Data Analysis

This section presents an analysis of key metrics surrounding Bitcoin's halving events, utilizing time series analysis to interpret patterns or trends in this data over time, providing a deeper understanding and insights into the dynamics. The analysis is partitioned into four distinct periods, each aligning with the occurrence of a halving event. Thus, Period 1 encompasses blocks 1 to 209,999, Period 2 covers blocks 210,000 to 419,999, Period 3 spans blocks 420,000 to 629,999, Period 4 includes data from blocks between 630,000 and 839,999, and Period 5 includes data from blocks between 840,000 and 855,833, as the subsequent halving event had not yet occurred at the time of this analysis. These events mark a significant milestone in Bitcoin's blockchain, where the block reward for miners is reduced by half approximately every 210,000 blocks. The delineation of these periods allows for a granular examination of how different phases of the halving events influence Bitcoin's transactional, economic, and market dynamics. We referenced Bitcoin's mainnet for block data (Transaction, Network Difficulty, and Reward) and utilised Investing.com data for cryptocurrency price and trading volume data.

4.1 Key Metrics

This section covers a statistical analysis of key metrics data related to Bitcoin.

Table 1. Key Metrics Associated with Bitcoin Halving Events: Data Period - 3rd January 2009 to 7th August 2024

Metrics	Period 1	Period 2	Period 3	Period 4	Period 5
SUM(TX)	9M	132M	388M	462M	-
AVG(TX)	44	629	1,846	2,199	4,093
AVG(D)	697K	41,762M	5,237G	34,947G	84,107G
AVG(R)	50.04	25.18	13.28	6.63	3.50
AVG(F)	0.04	0.18	0.78	0.38	0.37
AVG(C)	5	343	5,764	32,829	64,235
AVG(V)	41,320	48,827	640,231	42,225,260	66,691

From the provided key metrics in Table 1, several insightful observations can be made:

- **Transaction Count (SUM(TX))**: The consistent increase in total transaction count across different periods reflects a strong adoption and utilization of the Bitcoin network. This growth can be attributed to several factors, including increased acceptance by merchants, heightened awareness among users, and the implementation of scalability solutions such as the Lightning Network. The transaction count exhibited a dramatic increase, with a growth rate of approximately 4,211% from Period 1 to Period 3, highlighting the expanding use of the Bitcoin network. This substantial growth indicates that Bitcoin is becoming more widely used and integrated into various transactions. Since the most recent halving event occurred during period 5, there are fewer cases for analysis. Therefore, SUM(TX) has been excluded from the dataset for this period.

- **Average Transactions per Block (AVG(TX))**: The significant surge in average transactions per block indicates heightened network activity and efficient block space utilization. Factors influencing this surge include the adoption of Segregated Witness (SegWit) and optimized transaction batching strategies. The average transactions per block rose dramatically, with a growth rate of approximately 4,195% from Period 1 to Period 3. This growth also reflects increased user engagement and the network's ability to process more transactions per block.
- **Average Network Difficulty (AVG(D))**: The exponential growth in network difficulty underscores escalating competition among miners. This surge is linked to the proliferation of advanced mining hardware, improved mining pool efficiency, and miners' pursuit of higher profitability. Network difficulty experiences substantial growth, with an increase of approximately 5,013,916% from Period 1 to Period 4.
- **Average Block Reward (AVG(R))**: The consistent reduction in average block reward including transaction fees is in line with the scheduled subsidy halving events, which are designed to create scarcity and control the supply of Bitcoin.Although the average block reward steadily decreased by approximately 93% from Period 1 to Period 5, the corresponding rise in cryptocurrency prices more than offset this reduction. As a result, from a monetary perspective, the real value of the reward actually increased. This demonstrates that despite the halving events reducing the block reward, the significant price appreciation of Bitcoin continues to provide strong incentives for miners, influencing their strategies and operational decisions
- **Average Transaction Fees (AVG(F))**: Although transaction fees currently constitute a minor portion of total rewards, their perceived value has escalated in tandem with rising cryptocurrency prices. The variability in average transaction fees reflects the dynamic nature of the fee market, with a notable increase observed across three distinct periods. Conversely, the fourth and fifth periods exhibited stagnation in transaction fees, likely linked to the increases in cryptocurrency prices. While transaction fees still account for a relatively small percentage of overall rewards, the actual value that miners derive from these fees has markedly intensified due to the appreciation in cryptocurrency prices.
- **Average Cryptocurrency Price (AVG(C))**: The substantial appreciation in the average cryptocurrency price, especially from Period 1 to Period 3, indicates a marked increase in investor interest and speculative demand. Driven by macroeconomic factors, institutional adoption, and extensive media coverage, the average cryptocurrency price saw an extraordinary growth rate of approximately 1,187,600% from Period 1 to Period 5. This significant increase in price is crucial for maintaining miner profitability, particularly in the context of reduced block rewards due to halving events. The dramatic rise in average cryptocurrency price reflects the growing market value and under-

scores its role as a critical factor in supporting the financial viability of mining activities amidst changing reward structures.

- **Average Trading Volume Trends (AVG(V))**: The variations in average trading volume reveal a substantial increase, particularly notable in Period 3. This significant rise in trading activity suggests a surge in market engagement, which is influenced by the third halving event and related market dynamics. The average trading volume increased dramatically from Period 1 to Period 4, indicating a substantial boost in market activity and liquidity during this period. This heightened trading volume reflects increased investor participation and market interest, further contributing to the overall dynamics of the cryptocurrency market during the observed periods. However, in Period 5, the trading volume showed a downward trend, returning to levels seen before Period 2, suggesting a decline in market activity and reduced investor engagement compared to earlier periods.

The substantial increase in transaction count and average transactions per block reflects growing adoption of Bitcoin, driven by increasing user engagement and transaction activity. However, further analysis of market stability and efficiency would be needed to assess market maturity

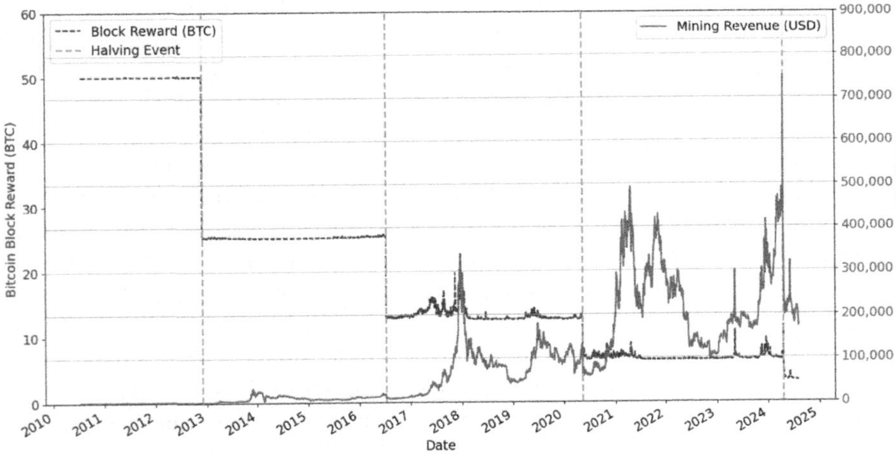

Fig. 3. Impact of Bitcoin Halving Events on Block Reward and Mining Incentives. This figure shows how the scheduled halving events reduced block rewards by 50%, while rising Bitcoin prices significantly increased mining incentives, particularly after the 2016 halving

The consistent growth of the Bitcoin ecosystem highlights its maturation and development over time, driven by the adoption of scaling solutions and enhancements in infrastructure. These advancements have significantly improved the network's ability to handle increasing transaction volumes. As block rewards decrease due to halving events, miners are increasingly relying on transaction fees to sustain their operations, a trend that became particularly evident in the fee market dynamics of Period 3.

The correlation between rising cryptocurrency prices and halving periods highlights the critical role of price appreciation in maintaining miner profitability despite reduced block rewards. However, the lag between revenue peaks and halving events varies across different cycles. Notably, in the most recent halving, the revenue peak appeared to align with the event, followed by a significant drop. This creates a self-reinforcing cycle where higher prices further incentivise mining activities, supporting the network's overall economic health.

In summary, the observed trends reflect a complex interplay of technological advancements, economic factors, and market dynamics that are shaping the evolution of the Bitcoin network. Despite the challenges posed by diminishing block rewards, the ongoing growth of the ecosystem demonstrates its resilience and adaptability to evolving conditions.

4.2 Mining Revenue Variation

The absolute Bitcoin subsidy awarded to miners has been reduced by fifty percent on four separate occasions due to the scheduled halving events. This reduction is part of a designed mechanism to control the money supply of Bitcoin and maintain its scarcity. However, as illustrated in Fig. 3, a conspicuous trend emerges showing that the Mining Incentive-calculated as the product of the Block Reward and Cryptocurrency Price-experienced a significant surge following the second halving event in 2016.

Despite the reduction in block rewards, the substantial increase in cryptocurrency prices led to a notable rise in Mining Incentives. This halving increase in Mining Incentives not only offset the effect of reduced block rewards but also surpassed the levels observed during the second halving event. This phenomenon can be attributed to several factors:

- **Cryptocurrency Price Surge**: The dramatic increase in cryptocurrency prices translates into higher monetary compensation for miners, effectively mitigating the impact of reduced block rewards. The appreciation in Bitcoin's price can compensate for the lower block reward.
- **Market Maturity and Adoption**: Following the second halving event, there was a significant increase in market maturity and adoption. This growth in user base and market engagement contributed to higher cryptocurrency prices.
- **Historical Price Dynamics**: Historically, Bitcoin halving events have been associated with increased price pressure due to the reduction in new supply. This price pressure can lead to a rise in Mining Incentives as higher prices drive up the overall compensation for miners, despite the halving.

In summary, while the halving events reduce the absolute block rewards received by miners, the concurrent rise in cryptocurrency prices has a substantial impact on Mining Incentives. This phenomenon highlights the complex interplay between block rewards, market dynamics, and cryptocurrency prices. To fully understand the economic implications for miners, it is essential to consider not only the reduction in block rewards but also the influence of market conditions and price fluctuations on overall compensation.

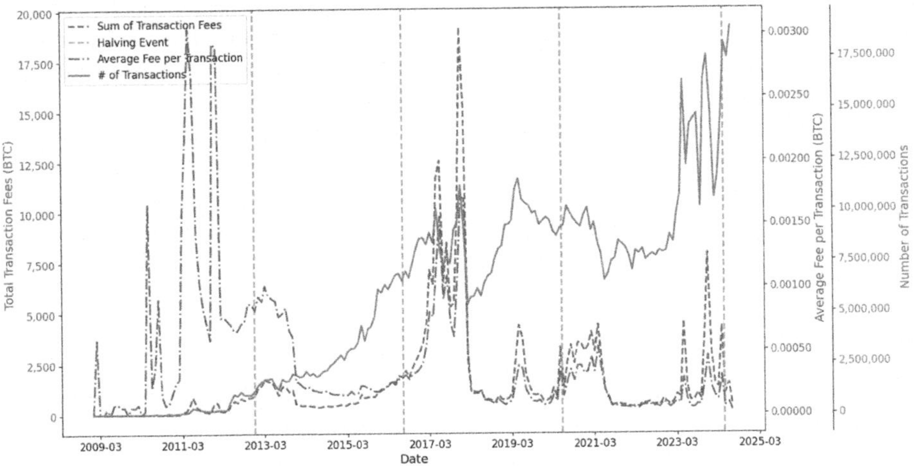

Fig. 4. Trends in Bitcoin Monthly Transaction Volume and Fees. This figure shows fluctuations in transaction volume and fees during halving events, emphasizing the growing importance of fees as Bitcoin issuance decreases

4.3 Transaction Fees Variation

During the halving events of November 2012, July 2016, May 2020, and April 2024, a noticeable increase in transaction volume was initially observed. The first two halving events were marked by a significant rise in trading volume. However, from the third halving event onward, a shift in the trend became apparent, with transaction volumes showing a tendency to decrease and stabilize. This trend is also evident in the associated transaction fees, as depicted in Fig. 4. This observation highlights the growing importance of transaction fees due to the reduced issuance of newly mined bitcoins.

- **Changes in Transaction Count and Fees**: An analysis of the dataset reveals a consistent upward trend in transaction count over time. In contrast, transaction fees did not follow a similar upward trajectory. While occasional increases in fees were noted, these changes were not particularly pronounced or sustained.
- **Average Fee per Transaction**: Following each halving event, there was some increase in the average fee per transaction. However, the overall trend did not demonstrate a significant or consistent rise, indicating that the impact of halving events on average fees was limited.

- **Yearly Trends**: Annual analysis of the data shows a steady increase in transaction count. Conversely, transaction fees exhibited considerable variability, with no significant upward trend observed in specific years. This variability suggests that other factors influence fee fluctuations.
- **Fee-Price Relationship**: The data does not suggest a clear correlation between transaction fees and the market price of Bitcoin. Fluctuations in Bitcoin prices did not appear to have a substantial impact on transaction fees, indicating that factors other than price is influencing fee levels.

In summary, while transaction counts have demonstrated a clear upward trend, the behavior of transaction fees is more complex. There is no significant or consistent increase in fees, and no strong correlation with Bitcoin's market price is evident. The observed trends underscore the evolving dynamics of transaction fees in response to the reduced issuance of new bitcoins.

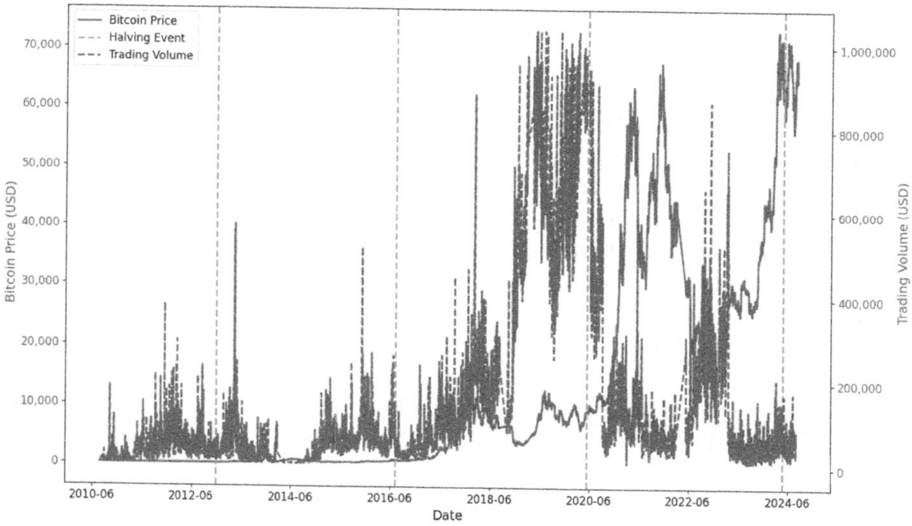

Fig. 5. Bitcoin Price and Trading Volume Trends Around Halving Events. The figure depicts Bitcoin's price and trading volume during the July 2016, May 2020, and April 2024 halvings. The July 2016 halving saw a clear price increase and higher trading volume, while the 2020 and 2024 halvings featured price rallies with more variable trading volumes

4.4 Cryptocurrency Price and Trading Volume Fluctuations

We analyzed the behavior of cryptocurrency prices and trading volume from [14] in relation to halving events, as depicted in Fig. 5.

- **Trading Volume and Price Uptrend (July 2016 halving)**: Bitcoin's price exhibited an upward trend, accompanied by increased trading volume. This aligns with the idea that the scarcity-induced price increase incentivised greater trading activity. The rise in trading volume during this period reflects heightened market interest and activity driven by the anticipation of future price increases.
- **Price Rally and Volatile Trading Volume (May 2020, Apr 2024 halving)**: The halving led to a notable price rally in Bitcoin. However, trading volume showed a distinct fluctuation pattern, alternating between periods of increase and decrease. This volatility can be attributed to the maturing Bitcoin market and the involvement of a larger and more diverse participant base. The oscillating trading volume, alongside the price surge, indicates that market participants' strategies and overall market dynamics played a significant role in shaping these fluctuations.

Halving events have a measurable impact on average trading volume. Period 2 shows a modest increase in trading volume, while Period 3 experiences a notable surge. This suggests that halving events can stimulate increased trading engagement and heightened market interest in Bitcoin, likely influenced by changes in supply dynamics and market sentiment. In contrast, Period 4 exhibits a decrease in average trading volume compared to the active Period 3, signaling a potential return to more typical trading activity levels. The average trading volume serves as an indicator of the market's responsiveness to halving events, capturing variations in trading activity and offering insights into shifts in market dynamics.

In summary, the analysis of these key metrics underscores the maturation of the Bitcoin ecosystem, characterized by consistent growth and adaptability. Enhanced scaling solutions and improved infrastructure have strengthened the network's capacity to handle increasing transaction volumes. The observed correlation between cryptocurrency prices and halving periods, where prices increased by up to 569% during the recent three halving event, highlights the critical role of price appreciation in sustaining miner profitability amid decreasing block rewards. This self-reinforcing cycle, driven by scarcity, demand, and a growing user base, contributes to Bitcoin's enduring resilience and robust market behavior.

5 Discussions

This section explores the landscape of halving events, building upon the data analysis presented earlier. It examines the prospective outlook on key metrics of mining revenue based on historical patterns and addresses strategic considerations for navigating the environment of decreasing subsidies.

5.1 Future Observations

With the April 2024 halving event now concluded, a comprehensive assessment of its implications for miners and the broader Bitcoin ecosystem is essential.

Analyzing the outcomes of this recent event alongside insights from previous halvings provides valuable perspectives on how it has impacted miner business models, network dynamics, transaction fees, cryptocurrency prices, and overall mining profitability.

5.1.1 Miner Business Model

The ongoing reduction in block rewards during halving events presents challenges to the traditional mining business model that relies heavily on subsidies. As illustrated in Fig. 3, effective compensation for miners has shown significant surges following past halving events. This trend suggests that miners have adeptly adapted to subsidy reductions by leveraging the increased value of Bitcoin. To remain profitable, miners must continually optimize their operations. Key strategies include:

- **Efficiency Improvements**: Investing in the latest mining hardware and technologies to enhance efficiency and hash rates is crucial. This investment maximizes the chances of successfully mining blocks and sustaining profitability.
- **Elastic Mining Model**: Developing dynamic mining profit management strategies is essential for energy-efficient blockchain mining. This approach involves systematic analysis of various factors influencing mining operations, aiding miners in making informed decisions for long-term sustainability and profitability.

5.2 Network Difficulty and Transaction Fee Dynamics

The consistent growth in average network difficulty observed during previous halving events indicates increased competition among miners. With reduced block rewards, miners are compelled to rely more on transaction fees to sustain profitability. This trend is expected to continue in future halving events.

To navigate this evolving landscape, miners and the broader community should consider:

- **Scalability Solutions**: The Bitcoin network must continue to explore and implement scalability solutions, such as the Lightning Network. These solutions enhance transaction throughput and reduce fees, contributing to a more sustainable fee market.
- **Flexible Fee Structures**: Mining pools and wallet providers could implement flexible fee structures that adapt to network conditions. Dynamic fee adjustments based on congestion levels can optimize both user experience and miner revenue.

5.3 Cryptocurrency Price and Market Dynamics

Historical data shows a clear correlation between cryptocurrency prices and halving events. The anticipation and aftermath of these events often coincide with significant price rallies. As we approach the 2024 halving event, it is crucial to consider the potential impact on market dynamics:

- **Market Sentiment**: The market's perception of the halving event plays a crucial role in price dynamics. Positive sentiment, driven by media coverage, institutional interest, and macroeconomic conditions, can contribute to price appreciation.
- **Risk Management**: Both investors and miners should implement robust risk management strategies. The volatile nature of cryptocurrency markets necessitates caution and preparedness for potential price fluctuations.
- **Macro Trends**: Monitoring broader economic trends, regulatory developments, and technological advancements is essential. External factors can influence cryptocurrency prices and market sentiment, impacting miner profitability.

5.3.1 Energy Cost and Sustainability

The environmental impact of Bitcoin mining has become a focal point for discussions and regulatory considerations. As the industry faces increased scrutiny, miners must proactively address sustainability concerns. Strategies for enhancing sustainability include:

- **Energy Cost Optimization**: Miners should consider transitioning to or increasing reliance on renewable energy sources [15], aligning with global sustainability goals. This not only contributes to environmental responsibility but also mitigates potential regulatory risks associated with carbon-intensive mining. Further, diversifying energy sources-such as renewables, dynamic wholesale energy, surplus energy utilization, and incorporating battery storage solutions-can enhance efficiency in blockchain mining operations.
- **Optimizing Mining Equipment Deployment**: Efficiently managing mining operations involves analyzing the revenue potential of various equipment, including ASICs, GPUs, and rigs, during block creation. This approach ensures strategic resource allocation to maximize efficiency and returns.

Balancing economic incentives, technological advancements, and sustainability is key to ensuring the continued growth and resilience of the Bitcoin network. The ability to adapt to changing conditions, implement innovative solutions, and foster a collaborative ecosystem will be pivotal in navigating the evolving landscape of cryptocurrency mining. As the industry matures, strategic decisions made in preparation for the 2024 halving event will shape Bitcoin's future trajectory and its role in the broader financial landscape. Future strategies discussed above will require significant attention and research from both academia and industry, and it is anticipated that such research efforts will play a crucial role in sustaining the growth and resilience of the Bitcoin network.

6 Conclusion and Future Works

Our investigation into Bitcoin's historical halving events reveals a pattern of maturation within the ecosystem, characterized by substantial growth in transaction count, network difficulty, and market activity surrounding these events. The conclusion of the April 2024 halving event has further solidified this trend, highlighting both the resilience of the Bitcoin network and the evolving strategies employed by miners. In the wake of the 2024 halving, miners have demonstrated their ability to adapt effectively to the reduction in block rewards. By capitalizing on Bitcoin's increasing value and enhancing operational efficiency, miners have managed to sustain and even enhance their profitability. This adaptability includes investments in cutting-edge mining hardware, dynamic profit management approaches, and a focus on sustainable energy practices. The aftermath of the 2024 halving underscores the need for strategic preparations as the Bitcoin ecosystem continues to evolve. Miners should prioritize efficiency improvements, diversify revenue sources, and adopt sustainable energy practices to navigate the reduced subsidy environment effectively.

Looking ahead, future research should focus on developing advanced optimization models for energy-efficient blockchain mining, including energy costs, equipment strategies, and renewable energy integration. Additionally, understanding the impact of scalability solutions, market sentiment, and regulatory developments on mining profitability will be essential. Research in these areas will help miners and industry participants adapt to future changes effectively.

In conclusion, the maturation of the Bitcoin network, demonstrated through its ability to adapt to subsidy reductions and evolving market conditions, highlights its resilience and enduring relevance. Strategic planning, innovation, and sustainability will be key factors in shaping Bitcoin's future trajectory and its broader impact on the financial landscape.

References

1. Nakamoto, S.: Bitcoin: A peer-to-peer electronic cash system. Decentralized business review (2008)
2. Meynkhard, A.: Fair market value of bitcoin: halving effect. Invest. Manage. Fin. Innov. **16**(4), 72 (2019)
3. Yi-Le Chan, J., Phoong, S.W., Phoong, S.Y., Cheng, W.K., Chen, Y.-L.: The bitcoin halving cycle volatility dynamics and safe haven-hedge properties: A msgarch approach. Mathematics **11**(3), 1–19 (2023)
4. Antoniadis, P., Martignoni, J.: 10 what could blockchain do for community networks. The community network manual: How to build the internet yourself, 223 (2018)
5. Croman, K., et al.: On scaling decentralized blockchains: (a position paper). In: Clark, J., Meiklejohn, S., Ryan, P.Y.A., Wallach, D., Brenner, M., Rohloff, K. (eds.) Financial Cryptography and Data Security: FC 2016 International Workshops, BITCOIN, VOTING, and WAHC, Christ Church, Barbados, February 26, 2016, Revised Selected Papers, pp. 106–125. Springer Berlin Heidelberg, Berlin, Heidelberg (2016). https://doi.org/10.1007/978-3-662-53357-4_8

6. Narayanan, A., Bonneau, J., Felten, E., Miller, A., Goldfeder, S.: Bitcoin and Cryptocurrency Technologies: a Comprehensive Introduction. Princeton University Press, ??? (2016)
7. Miers, I., Garman, C., Green, M., Rubin, A.D.: Zerocoin: Anonymous distributed e-cash from bitcoin. In: 2013 IEEE Symposium on Security and Privacy, pp. 397-411 (2013). IEEE
8. Huberman, G., Leshno, J.D., Moallemi, C.: Monopoly without a monopolist: an economic analysis of the bitcoin payment system. Rev. Econ. Stud. **88**(6), 3011–3040 (2021)
9. Kroll, J.A., Davey, I.C., Felten, E.W.: The economics of bitcoin mining, or bitcoin in the presence of adversaries. In: Proceedings of WEIS, vol. 2013 (2013). Citeseer
10. Wang, C., Chu, X., Qin, Y.: Measurement and analysis of the bitcoin networks: a view from mining pools. In: 2020 6th International Conference on Big Data Computing and Communications (BIGCOM), pp. 180–188 (2020). IEEE
11. Fantazzini, D., Kolodin, N.: Does the hashrate affect the bitcoin price? J. Risk Finan. Manage. **13**(11), 263 (2020)
12. Marthinsen, J.E., Gordon, S.R.: The price and cost of bitcoin. Q. Rev. Econ. Finan. **85**, 280–288 (2022)
13. Bejan, C.A., Bucerzan, D., Crăciun, M.D.: Bitcoin price evolution versus energy consumption; trend analysis. Appl. Econ. **55**(13), 1497–1511 (2023)
14. https://au.investing.com/crypto/bitcoin. Accessed 8 Aug 2024
15. Cho, D., Ramachandran, G., Jurdak, R., Kanhere, S.: Cost-aware blockchain mining strategy: Dynamic energy pricing (dep) model. In: Proceedings of the 6th Conference on Blockchain Research & Applications for Innovative Networks and Services, Berlin, Germany, October, 2024. (BRAINS'24) (2024)

Privacy Preserving Reputation System for Self-Sovereign Identity

Yu Yen Miffy Chung, Evan Krul, and Hye-Young Paik(✉)

School of Computer Science and Engineering, University of New South Wales, Sydney, Australia
{yu.chung,e.krul,h.paik}@unsw.edu.au

Abstract. Current identity management practices are proving to be increasingly insecure, invasive and overwhelming to both users and identity providers. Self-sovereign identity is an emerging model which focuses on giving users full control over their personal data without relying on third-party providers. This paper aims to examine how an additional human layer of trust can be incorporated into this model through the design of reputation system which aligns with the user-centric and privacy preserving principles of self-sovereign identity.

Keywords: digital identity · reputation · self-sovereign identity · trust

1 Introduction

Due to the increasing usage of online services, we are confronted with a growing amount of complex, inconsistent and insecure digital identity practices [16]. Current identity management models, which predominantly rely on centralised data repositories and identity providers, are suffering from a range of security, privacy and usability issues. Users are struggling to maintain control over different sets of credentials across services, identity providers are facing security attacks on their databases which can incur high costs and lead to reputation loss or identity fraud. Users are also often subject to invasion of privacy as they have little control and visibility over how their personal information is used, managed, shared or disposed by identity providers [16].

Hence decentralised identity, commonly blockchain-based, has emerged as a new approach to identity management. The SSI model uses DIDs and VCs to enable individuals to have full control over usage of personal data for a range of purposes beyond identity authentication or proofing certification [11]. Despite the processes in the model being technically secure, it lacks elements which help promote human trust, that is whether we can trust that involved entities are acting without malicious intent. This paper explores a way of building trust by constructing a reputation system which aligns with the principles of the SSI model to help build up this additional layer of trust.

S. Kanhere et al. (Eds.): SDLT 2024, CCIS 2453, pp. 55–70, 2025.
https://doi.org/10.1007/978-981-96-4442-1_4

2 Related Work and Problem Statement

2.1 Reputation Systems

Reputation can be considered as a collective measure of trustworthiness based on the referrals or ratings from members in a community [10]. Reputation systems are programs or algorithms that allow users to rate and or review one another, likely after the completion of a transaction, and often use the aggregated ratings to compute a reputation score (most commonly just the average). Since an individual's subjective sense of trust is commonly derived from a combination of received referrals and personal experience, reputation systems are effective in allowing users to assess the reliability of entities and quality of services before they decide to interact with the given entity [10]. Thus, it is likely that the implementation of a reputation system would be highly beneficial in building the layer of human trust in an SSI model. It would be additionally useful in scenarios where:

- The user and service provider are interacting for the first time. Since the user has no prior experience with the service provider, having access to a reputation score and or other user reviews can help influence their decision to trust, especially when the service provider is not well known. This is particularly applicable to peer-to-peer services (such as Uber, Airbnb, Ebay) where often the user will inter-act with different service providers every time they engage with the overall platform.
- Verifiers require additional information to be disclosed. For example, in a car sharing setting a car owner may want to see the car renter's history with other car sharing platforms on top of the basic credentials required such as a license to en-sure that the user is not involved with car fraud. Studies on trust and distrust on the web have highlighted how users are more willing to share information with service providers who possess a positive reputation which subsequently increases the chance for a successful transaction [15].

However, current reputation systems are mainly centralised and not privacy preserving which do not align with the principles of SSI. In a centralised system, users need to trust the service operator to maintain the correctness of the reputation scores as well as the privacy of sensitive data like payment history or addresses [17]. This trust can be easily abused by the central authority. Not preserving the anonymity of users who leave ratings can also lead to a range of negative consequences. For example, studies have demonstrated that vendors on eBay discriminate against customers based on their review/rating history [17]. Furthermore, if a vendor can link a rating/review with a transaction they may try to cause harm to the user in future transactions. Hence to avoid harassment, honest users may be deterred from submitting reviews or truthful reviews which negatively impacts the reliability of the reputation systems overall [14].

A challenge in implementing a decentralized and privacy preserving design is that it could leave the system vulnerable to threats including:

Self-promoting attacks: Service providers may falsely increase their own reputation. A typical example is a Sybil attack where an entity creates a large number of identities in the network, gaining disproportionately large influence and utilises them to boost their own reputation. In a network where users re-main anonymous, it would be highly difficult to ensure that feedback received is legitimate as its source is unknown [17]. Typically, sybil attacks are mitigated by having a central authority like certificate authorities to verify the identities of users by making it more difficult for users to access a service (for example requiring a phone number or license to be onboarded to a platform), linking a rating/review to a valid transaction or analysing behaviour and history recorded in the system to identity malicious users.

Whitewashing: This occurs when attackers exploit system vulnerabilities to improve or repair their reputation [8] by re-entering with a different identify and hence a renewed reputation.

Bad mouthing: Similar to self-promoting attacks, this occurs when one or more identities falsely provide negative feedback to another. Systems that do not verify feedback origin are highly vulnerable to such attacks [15].

Denial of Service: Attackers will prevent the calculation and distribution of reputation values, causing a denial of service. This is commonly done through over-loading the network or any computational resources [8].

Although defences against these attacks exist, many involve tracking user identities and behaviours, which contradicts SSI principles. Therefore, new methods and technologies are needed to achieve all desired qualities.

2.2 Problem Statement

While SSI management processes are cryptographically secure, the model lacks elements that promote human trust. This is evident in the interaction between a user and verifier, as confirming a verifier's identity alone is often insufficient for the user to trust that the service provider has no malicious intent and to willingly disclose their credentials.

Although there are no techniques that can guarantee honest human behaviour, elements can be integrated into the SSI model to help build the additional layer of trust that other system protocols do not address. Since "trust is not a decision, it is an ongoing process," and in real life, learning from shared experiences builds trust over time [12], reputation systems are likely an effective solution, as demonstrated by their widespread use in online environments. However, most existing reputation systems are not compatible with SSI, highlighting the need for an improved design that possesses these qualities:

- Decentralised: The system should be decentralised to avoid any central point of control or failure and not rely on any third parties, which must be trusted to behave without malicious intent.
- Privacy-Preserving: Ratings/reviews and user identities should not be linkable. More specifically, the system should enforce the unlinkability of transactions and ratings [14]. Ratings from the same customer should also remain

unlinkable, with only the ability to link a rating to a service provider. This ensures a fair and useful reputation system.
- Robustness: The system should be robust against threats, such as Sybil.

3 Background

We introduce the technical components necessary for our proposed system.

3.1 Self-sovereign Identity Model and Its Components

Self-sovereign identity (SSI) represents the latest evolution of identity management models. It is user-centric and decentralised, aiming to give identity holders better control over their personal data, with a strong emphasis on data portability and minimisation [1,16]. The implementation of SSI generally involves the following components.

Decentralised Identifiers (DIDs). DIDs are globally unique cryptographic identifiers managed by a decentralised infrastructure, such as a distributed ledger. Ownership of a DID can be proven using cryptographic proofs like digital signatures. The DID specification also distinguishes types of DIDs, including public DIDs (for interaction with an unknown number of entities) and pairwise DIDs (used in peer-to-peer connections without requiring a storage system) [11,16].

Verifiable Credentials (VCs). Verifiable credentials are data structures that represent cryptographically verifiable and tamper-proof claims, detailing qualifications, abilities, or authorities granted to an individual (e.g., information found in a passport, license, or bank account ownership). A VC may include details such as issuer information, claim expiry date, a public key for verification, or the revocation mechanism [18].

Trust Triangle and DIDComm. The main roles in the SSI model include: (1) *Identity holders* (users) who control how their credentials are managed and shared, (2) *Identity providers* (issuers) authorised to issue credentials, which can be official entities like government organisations, financial institutions, any organisation, or even users themselves, and (3) *Identity verifiers* who verify credentials, ensuring they come from a competent issuer, are tamper-evident, and remain relevant [7]. Figure 1 illustrates how the components and actors in the system function together. All actors can generate and control personal DIDs; users store and manage their verifiable credentials using crypto wallets, and service providers can verify credentials using public key cryptography anchored on a distributed ledger [13]. The relationship between these entities forms a textbftrust triangle: the issuer trusts the user, the user trusts the verifier, and the verifier trusts the issuer. In the interaction between an identity holder (user) and a verifier (service provider), secure peer-to-peer communication is necessary for the exchange and verification of credentials. This communication can be facilitated using DID Communication (DIDComm), an encrypted, DID-based protocol developed as part of the Hyperledger Aries project.

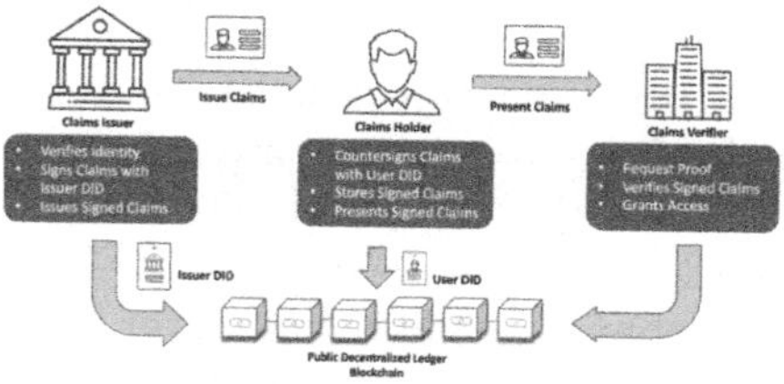

Fig. 1. Roles and information flow involved in the SSI model [9]

Figure 2 shows an example of DIDComm between two individuals, Alice and Bob. Alice wishes to communicate with Bob, so she resolves Bob's DID document to obtain his endpoint and public key for their relationship. She then encrypts the message using Bob's public key and adds authentication with her private key before sending it. Bob receives and decrypts the message, authenticating the sender using Alice's public key from her DID document [5]. This protocol allows peers to communicate directly through secure messages by utilising information from the DID document, such as the public key and its associated endpoint. It also supports mutual authentication helping to prevent issues like man-in-the-middle attacks and credential theft [11].

Alice has a secret key (sk_a), a DID Document for Bob which contains an endpoint ($endpoint_{bob}$), and a public key (pk_b).
Bob has a secret key (sk_b), a DID Document for Alice which contains Alice's public key (pk_a).
Alice encrypts the plain text message (m) using pk_b, creates cipher text (ct_b).
Alice signs ct_b using sk_a to create a signature (σ).
Alice sends (ct_b,σ) to $endpoint_{bob}$.
Bob verifies σ using pk_a.
if *(Verified)* **then**
    Bob decrypts ct_b using sk_b.
    Bob reads m.
end

Fig. 2. Example of DIDComm [11]

3.2 Blind Signatures

Blind signatures are a form of digital signatures which can enhance privacy by allowing an individual to obtain a signature from a signer on a message without the signer learning anything about the contents of the message [6]. It is useful in schemes where anonymity is desired and can provide: *(1) Unlinkability:* the signer cannot link the signed message to the signing session nor the user on whose behalf they signed. *(2) Blindness:* the signer cannot learn about a user's message. *(3) Unforgeability:* the signature cannot be falsified, as it is ensured that at most n signatures are produced after n interactions between a user and signer.

The Chaum blind signature scheme is simple and is based on the RSA signature scheme. From the RSA signature scheme, we can assume that the public key is in the form (n, e) where $n = pq$ (p, q are safe RSA prime numbers) and e is a prime between 2^{16} and $(p-1)(q-1)$. The corresponding private key is given by (p, q, d) where the signing exponent $d = e^{-1} \mod ((p-1)(q-1))$ [2].

When a user wants to obtain a blind signature for some message m, they will choose a blinding factor $r \in \mathbb{Z}_n$ and compute the blinded hash of the key and blinding factor $m' = H(m)r^e(\mod (n))$ where $H(\cdot)$ is a hash function. This is sent to a signer and they will sign m' with their private key producing $s = m'^d \mod (n)$, which is sent back to the user. The user can then unblind s to obtain the signature on m by computing $s' = sr^{-1} \mod (n)$ [4]. This signature is valid for the message since:

$$s' = sr^{-1} = m'^d r^{-1} = (H(m)r^e)^d r^{-1} = H(m)^d r^{ed} r^{-1} = H(m)^d \mod (n)$$

Thus, using this process, a user is able to obtain a valid signed message proving that they were involved in an interaction with the signer while preserving the privacy of their identity and the contents of the message [4].

4 System Design Overview

4.1 Reputation System Design

The solution utilises both the Ethereum blockchain and blind signatures to achieve a decentralised and privacy preserving reputation system design. In this system, Ethereum tokens serve as a mean for service providers to receive reviews. Chaums blind signature scheme will be used to create review tokens which will be necessary for users to submit a review. The system will also create a new smart contract for each service provider which will store records of reputation data and token balance while full details and other relevant information will be stored off chain.

Smart Contracts - the system uses three smart contracts. All state changing functions in the contracts will restrict usage permission with modifiers which will only allow the system owner to access those functionalities.

Service Provider Contract: This contract is used to record reputation data associated with a service provider. This includes an overall rating, a list of hashed textual reviews, balance of Ethereum ERC-20 tokens and a list of received review tokens. The review data is hashed to reduce storage, but its record ensures any tampering with off chain data can be traced. The Ethereum tokens are consumed (transferred to the factory contract) upon giving out a review token to a user and later when receiving a review from a user the review token is stored to prevent double use of tokens.

Factory Contract: This contract follows a factory design pattern and will create a new Service Provider Contract instance every time a new service provider joins the system. A contract registry which is a mapping between the service provider ID and contract address is also stored in this contract. This contract is also responsible for randomly distributing Ethereum tokens to service provider contracts when a new re-view is given to the system. It is important to note that the random choice of who receives the Ethereum token is generated off chain and only the transfer of tokens to the chosen service provider is completed on chain. This is because smart contracts are deterministic and deployed publicly hence if any user is able to determine how values are randomised, they will be able to predict the result and exploit this knowledge to their advantage. Despite this, the transfer of tokens will still be controlled by logic implemented in smart contracts allowing for any biased or unauthorised transfers to be traced and detected if necessary.

ERC-20 Token Contract: This contract simply creates the Ethereum tokens necessary for the system.

User Review Token and Protocol – The review token is given to a user after they participate in a valid transaction with a service provider. Here is the process by which it is generated using Chaums blind signature scheme (Fig. 3):

procedure ACQUIRE_TOKEN $(s, pubKey, e, n, x)$ $\Delta(e, n)$ is the service provider's public RSA key pair, x the identifier of the transaction
$m_1 \leftarrow hash\ (pubKey)$ $\Delta($ $hash$ is a cryptographic hash function such as sha256R
$r \leftarrow \text{rand}int(0, n)$
$m_1 \leftarrow m_1 r^e$
send$((m_1, x), s)$
return (m_1, r)
procedure ISSUE_TOKEN(c, m_1, d, n, x) $\Delta($ (n, d) is the service provider's private **RSA** key pair
if verify(x) $then$ Δ the has to specify **Verify**
$\bar{t}y \leftarrow m_1^d mod\ n$
send$(\bar{t}y, c)$
return $\bar{t}$ such as $sha256R$
procedure UN_BLIND_TOKEN$(\bar{t}y, r, e, n)$
$t \leftarrow \bar{t}yr^{-1}\ mod\ n$
return t

Fig. 3. Token Related Functions implemented using Chaums [14]

The system will generate a random hash string and send this to the user. Note that it is important that this string cannot be revealed to the service provider at this point. This string will be referred to as the *review key*. This key will either need to be copied to a secure location or can be downloaded as a VC, which can be stored in a digital wallet for later use. The review key will then be blinded by the system using the service provider's public RSA key (which is already known by the system, likely stored in the system's off-chain database) and sent to the service provider.

The service provider will sign this blinded review key using their private RSA key before uploading it back to the system. This signing is done external to the system by the service provider themselves.

The system will then unblind the signed blinded review key using the provider's public RSA key again and send this to the user. This unblinded signed review key is the *review token* and, again, will either need to be copied to a secure location or can be downloaded as a VC, which can be stored in a digital wallet for later use.

Later on, when a user wishes to submit a review against a service provider, they will also need to submit the review token and review key that they received. The validity of the review token will be cryptographically verified using the service provider's public RSA key and the review key. This ensures that reviews can only be submitted for valid transactions whilst preserving user privacy. The sequence diagram Fig. 4 shows the system's general protocol.

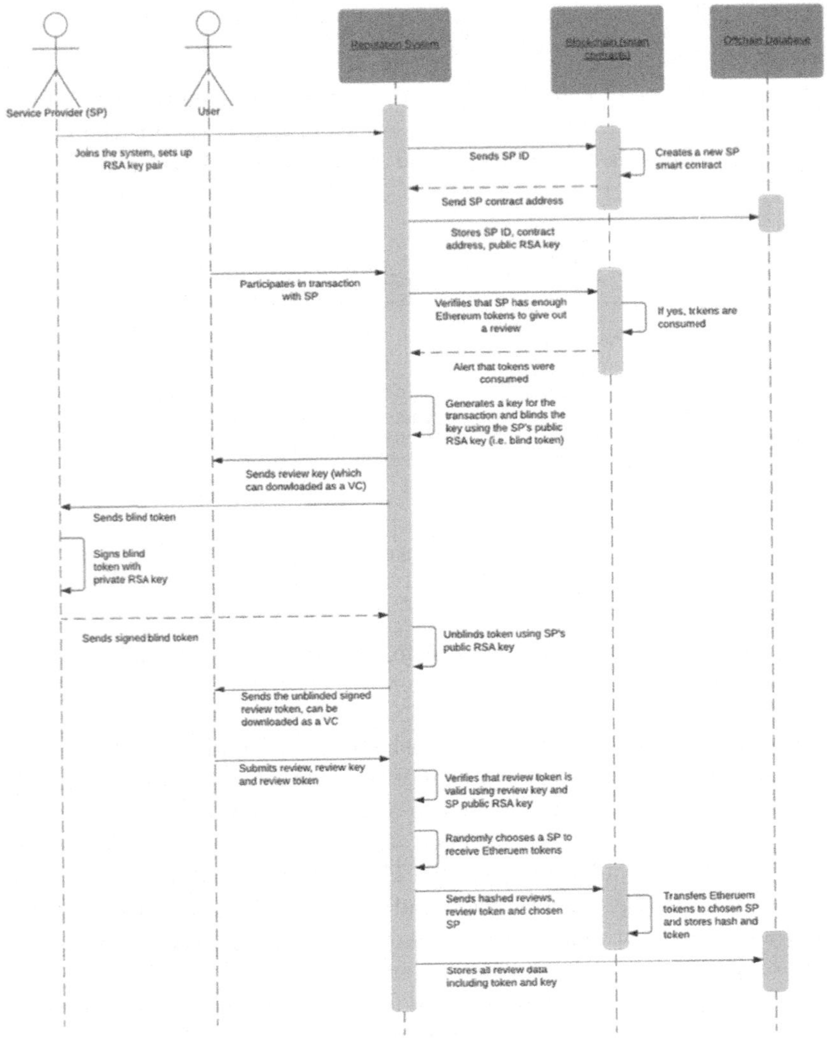

Fig. 4. Review Protocol Overview

Reputation Verifiable Credential. Service providers can have their reputation score issued as a verifiable credential. The credential subject will include their ID, average rating, and service provider smart contract address. This functionality allows their reputation to become more portable and can be verified by other companies or interested individuals. It also allows them to selectively disclose their reputation information to others if they wish to do so.

5 Implementation

We have implemented the reputation system design, with a minimalistic web interface. Figure 5 shows the architecture with the main languages and libraries used at each layer. The implementation code is available at GitHub[1]. The main functionalities of the system include:

- Registering/Logging in as a user or service provider.
- Service provider RSA key setup.
- Transaction between service provider and user.
- User reviewing a service provider.
- Viewing reputation data associated with a service provider.

5.1 Blockchain

The smart contracts were written using Solidity and were compiled and deployed using Hardhat, an Ethereum development environment.

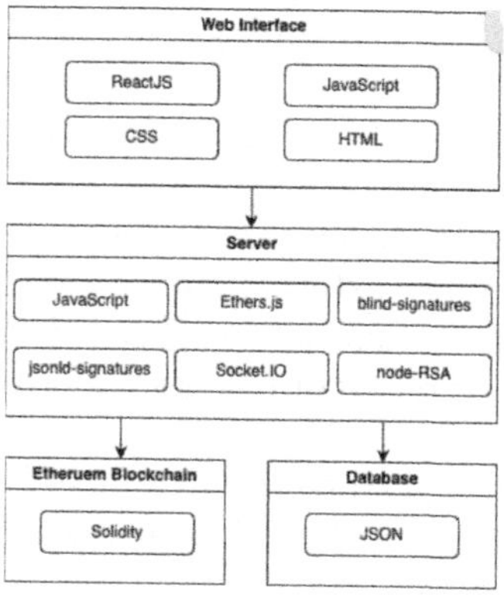

Fig. 5. Implementation architecture

The contracts were deployed to the Sepolia testnet, which uses a proof-of-stake consensus mechanism to mimic the current Ethereum mainnet. All interaction with the blockchain was completed through one Ethereum user account,

[1] https://github.com/miffy-c/Thesis-Demo-System/tree/main.

and test ether was obtained using the Ethereum Sepolia Faucet. Sepolia was chosen since it is a relatively younger testnet (compared to Goerli) with fewer deployed applications, allowing for faster syncing and reduced storage requirements to run a node [19]. Additionally, Sepolia test ether is easily obtainable at no cost. Finally, tools like Etherscan were used to help track smart contract transactions.

5.2 Frontend and Backend

React JS, Bootstrap, and Material UI libraries were used to build a user-friendly and intuitive web interface. The Socket.IO library was also used to facilitate communication between the frontend and backend, which was necessary during the review token generation process.

The backend of the system was written entirely in JavaScript, and Express, a Node.js web application framework, was used to develop the backend server of the web app. Since the off-chain database of this demo system is not of much relevance, a JSON file was used to store any data not uploaded to the chain.

Infura, which provides straightforward Ethereum network APIs, was used to connect to the Sepolia testnet. The Ethers.js library was then used to interact with smart contracts and send transactions. Although, in comparison, web3.js is a more popular library for building decentralised applications, there were issues with communicating with contract functions that had modifiers, and hence Ethers.js was used instead.

To generate the review tokens, both the Blind Signature JavaScript library and the Node RSA library were used. The Node RSA library was used to generate RSA key pairs in PEM format as well as export and import keys given input in a PEM string format. This was necessary as part of the 'key setup' and 'signing' processes for the service provider. The Blind Signature library was used for blinding, signing, unblinding, and verifying, given the user review token and the service provider's RSA key pair.

Although generating an RSA key pair and signing the blinded token by the service provider must be done external to the system due to privacy issues, downloadable files with instructions are provided through the interface and can be easily run if desired. The screenshot below shows the key generation file, which outputs an RSA key pair; the public key should be uploaded to the interface, while the private key should be stored safely.

Figure 6 shows `ReviewKeyCredential`, which would be issued to a user after a valid transaction with a service provider and would contain the service provider ID and review key, as shown in the `credentialSubject`.

```
{
  "@context": [
    "https://www.w3.org/2018/credentials/v1",
    "https://w3id.org/demoSystem/v1"
  ],
  "id": "http://example.edu/credentials/1872",
  "type": [
    "VerifiableCredential",
    "ReviewKeyCredential"
  ],
  "issuer": "https://example.edu/issuers/demoSystem",
  "issuanceDate": "2023-11-18T13:26:29.410Z",
  "credentialSubject": {
    "serviceProvider": "hunter",
    "reviewKey": "c6c5da0a7950fbc732a943fe867b9f69d819371a"
  },
  "proof": {
    "type": "Ed25519Signature2018",
    "created": "2023-11-18T13:26:29.410Z",
    "verificationMethod": "https://example.edu/issuers/keys/1",
    "proofPurpose": "assertionMethod",
    "jws":
"eyJhbGciOiJFZERTQSIsImI2NCI6ZmFsc2UsImNyaXQiOlsiYjY0Il19..IiwBNXJ9LOXBT3SYWIYp2U6wJf1D
JiO9b2nLscbxf6kuLgRQL7wZrzcARsLiaBrqMsPU-jRdbsegybFoPJKhCA"
  }
}
```


Fig. 6. An example of ReviewKeyCredential

6 Evaluation

6.1 Gas Usage and Optimisation

Gas refers to the unit that measures the computational effort required to execute specific operations on EVM blockchains. Thus, it is vital to optimise smart contracts to prioritise cost-efficient actions and avoid expensive ones to reduce overall gas consumption. This will lead to lower transaction costs and improved efficiency, ultimately providing a more affordable and accessible blockchain experience for users [3].

In order to estimate gas usage and test functionality, unit tests were written for all smart contract functions. Below is a screenshot of a gas report generated from the tests (Fig. 7).

Solc version: 0.8.19		Optimizer enabled: false		Runs: 200	Block limit: 30000000 gas	
Methods		17 gwei/gas			1835.31 usd/eth	
Contract	Method	Min	Max	Avg	# calls	usd (avg)
ReputationFactory	createServiceProvider	1978271	1978331	1978326	31	61.72
ServiceProvider	createUserToken	41828	63728	53809	16	1.67
ServiceProvider	sendReview	144710	161810	158390	5	4.94
Deployments					% of limit	
ReputationFactory		-	-	4438684	14.8 %	138.49
ServiceProvider		-	-	2110967	7 %	65.86

Fig. 7. Gas fees and costs

A major way to reduce gas costs is to minimise contract storage, as both reading from and writing to storage incur high gas costs. Hence, in this system, the least possible amount of data is stored on-chain, and only minimal records of data are kept as a means to trace any tampering with data off-chain. Using fixed-size variables, as opposed to dynamic ones, is also considerably less expensive, so textual review data, which is the largest data in the system, is hashed and stored in a `byte32` array.

Furthermore, mappings are much more efficient and inexpensive compared to arrays, which are packable but iterative. As a result, it is only recommended to use arrays over mappings when looping is absolutely necessary, or when it is possible to pack the data types. Therefore, only the hashed reviews were stored in an array, and all other data, such as review tokens and the contract registry, are stored in a mapping. Additionally, no iteration is ever required in the contracts, but if necessary, the reviews array can be retrieved and iterated over off-chain. Using the correct data types also helps reduce usage, such as using the `constant` keyword for the token consumption limit.

Another major way to optimise gas usage is to avoid external function calls (i.e., calling functions from other contracts). Initially, the smart contracts were written so that all calls to the service provider contract functions would be done through the factory contract. Essentially, the factory contract would act as a controller, and it would only be necessary to connect to one contract in the backend for convenience. However, this would mean all calls would be external calls, costing approximately (the amount always varies) an extra 2000–3000 gas in comparison to the same direct call.

The current implementation, however, connects directly to the specified service provider contract to make calls. Although this design does cost more gas initially since the Service Provider Contract also needs to be deployed in the backend to obtain the contract ABI, which allows us to connect to it, this extra deployment cost is a one-off expense and likely does not compare to the accumulation of extra gas costs if only external calls were made.

6.2 Performance Execution Time

Five measurements of the execution time of three major system functionalities were taken. All three functionalities involve calling at least one function from the smart contracts and were chosen as appropriate tasks to measure.

Table 1. Results of 5 runs (in seconds)

Functionality	r1	r2	r3	r4	r5	avg (s)
Registering a Service Provider	13.56	14.62	20.03	32.54	17.87	19.78
Creating a Review Token	21.85	12.39	10.97	18.09	8.82	14.42
Submitting a Review	5.58	20.71	16.45	17.78	15.32	15.17

Table 1 shows that there is a relatively large range in time for all three functionalities, likely due to blockchain network traffic. The averages between all three functionalities are quite similar, with registering a service provider being slightly higher, likely because the function call involves deploying a new service provider contract. Overall, the average execution time needed for all functionalities does not exceed 20 s, which is acceptable, as the average Ethereum block time is 12 s.

However, as the number of system users increases, methods to optimise sending multiple transactions simultaneously will be needed. Deploying the contracts on the mainnet rather than the testnet will also likely improve execution time, as it processes a higher frequency of transactions, has larger numbers of nodes, and more developed interfaces.

6.3 Analysis of Solution Design

User Privacy. User anonymity and review unlinkability are both guaranteed in this system. Service providers, when given a review, are unable to distinguish the identity of the user (and transaction) who submitted this review. This is because, for each transaction, the service provider will know the user's identity, any transaction data, and a blinded view of the review key. While a review from a user will contain the service provider's identity, any review data, the review key, and the review token (i.e., unblinded view of the signed review key). Since, for each transaction, the system generates a new review key that is not stored or revealed to the service provider during the transaction stage, the key is entirely independent of the user's identity.

Additionally, the blind signature scheme guarantees that the review token is unlinkable with the blinded view of the review key shown to the service provider during the transaction. For these reasons, it is also not possible to determine whether two reviews are given by the same user, given that the review key is truly randomly generated. Note that since the review key and token are both not recorded by the system until after the submission of a review, the system is also unable to link a user's identity or transaction to a review.

Service Provider Privacy. The privacy of the service provider is protected by restricting permission to view their reputation data. To view the full data, users must be registered in the system, as only the average reputation score and hashed reviews are stored on the public blockchain. Permission to call functions in smart contracts is also restricted using modifiers to prevent the public from tampering with the data. Individuals external to the system who wish to view reputation data can only do so through the service provider (from VC), who has the choice to selectively disclose information.

Malicious Behaviour. This system prioritises preventing malicious actions from service providers, and thus one challenge to this system is how to prevent this kind of behaviour from users, such as bad-mouthing. To begin with, it is rather difficult to detect malicious user behaviour since there are no means to differentiate between a genuinely negative transaction or experience and deliberate bad feedback. However, some ways to help avoid such scenarios include giving out the review token *after* a transaction. If the token is given out before a valid transaction finishes, the system can be easily exploited by malicious individuals, such as competing service providers. This type of incident would be difficult to detect and prevent, especially since users are anonymous. On the other hand, if the token is given out after the transaction, it is possible for the service provider to withhold the token and prevent a review despite completing the transaction. However, this scenario is comparatively easier to detect, as service providers can be identified and held accountable.

Another method to minimise the effect of malicious user behaviour is to perform data analysis on numerical reputation values, such as outlier detection, calculation of median, range, and standard deviation, to give users a less biased view of reputation data associated with a service provider. Finally, it is likely that a privacy-preserving and secure system will help encourage users to give truthful reviews more frequently.

Defence Against Attacks. Self-Promoting/Sybil Attacks/Denial of Service: Service providers are unable to create limitless identities to disrupt the system since they need to spend Ethereum tokens to give review tokens, of which they have a limited number. Additionally, there is no way of controlling how often they receive Ethereum tokens since they are randomly distributed after the submission of a review. There is also no means by which the service providers can buy the fungible tokens.

Whitewashing: There is not much merit for service providers to leave and re-enter the system since the initial reputation score is 0. However, if a provider has accumulated very negative feedback, they may believe starting over would be easier. To prevent this, the service provider ID can be bound to a credential or address that is difficult to change or replace. For instance, their identity can be their public DID or an endpoint to an interface they own.

Bad Mouthing: This is partially mitigated by the requirement of review tokens, as they are only issued after a valid transaction occurs. However, it cannot completely prevent such attacks. Other mechanisms that help decrease the occurrence and impact of bad-mouthing are described in the 'Malicious Actions' section above.

7 Future Work

Blind Signature Scheme Using ECDSA

The blind signature scheme used in this implementation requires RSA keys; hence, the key pair generation and signing needed to be done external to the system. This is quite tedious, and it would be ideal if the blind signatures could be created using the key pair associated with an Ethereum account. In this way, service providers would only need to connect their Ethereum account to the system, and actions like signing could simply be done through a wallet extension like MetaMask.

However, currently, most blockchains, including Ethereum, use the Elliptic Curve Digital Signature Algorithm (ECDSA) to generate their keys, and there does not appear to be any well-known and well-tested implementation of a blind signature scheme using this algorithm. If such a scheme could be developed, it would allow this system to be better integrated with blockchain and more user-friendly.

Further Integration with SSI

Many aspects of the reputation system can also be altered to further integrate with elements of the Self-Sovereign Identity (SSI) model. For example, currently, service providers and users are identified by their emails, but this can be replaced with a Decentralised Identifier (DID). This would allow processes like the transaction to occur using the DIDComm protocol, which would help improve the overall security of the system.

8 Conclusion

The significance of SSI will only grow with the increasing usage of online services and the growing frequency of security attacks and privacy issues. As with any identity management model, it is vital to consider what additional mechanisms can be put in place to fulfil the trust requirements of the system. From analysing the interactions involved with SSI, we can see that, although the protocols are cryptographically secure, they lack elements that promote human trust.

A common yet effective way to build trust in online environments is through reputation systems, but most current designs do not align with SSI principles. A solution that utilises the Ethereum blockchain and smart contracts, as well as Chaum's blind signature scheme, was proposed and implemented as a simple web interface. Through a detailed security and performance analysis, it was demonstrated how the reputation system is mainly decentralised and privacy-preserving while being robust to attacks.

Thus, this demonstrates its potential as a mechanism for improving trust, especially human trust, in a decentralised identity management model.

References

1. Allen, C.: The path to self-sovereign identity (2016). http://www.lifewithalacrity.com/2016/04/the-path-to-self-sovereign-identity.html. Accessed 30 Feb 2023
2. Bleumer, G.: Chaum blind signature scheme. In: Encyclopedia of Cryptography and Security, pp. 199–200 (2011). https://doi.org/10.1007/978-1-4419-5906-5_185, https://doi.org/10.1007/978-1-4419-5906-5_185
3. CertiK: Gas optimization in ethereum smart contracts: 10 best practices (2023). https://certik.medium.com/gas-optimization-in-ethereum-smart-contracts-10-best-practices-cbd57548bdf0. Accessed 22 September 2023

4. Chami, R.: On blind signatures for untraceable payments by David Chaum (2020). https://medium.com/@chamirachid/on-blind-signatures-for-untraceable-payments-by-david-chaum-275bbd6e1546. Accessed 26 April 2023
5. DIDComm: Didcomm messaging v2.x editor's draft. https://identity.foundation/didcomm-messaging/spec/. Accessed 14 Mar 2023
6. Fernàndez-València, R.: Blind signatures (2022). https://medium.com/iovlabs-innovation-stories/blind-signatures-af6338da6347, medium. Innovation Stories
7. Grüner, A., Mühle, A., Gayvoronskaya, T., Meinel, C.: A comparative analysis of trust requirements in decentralized identity management. In: Barolli, L., Takizawa, M., Xhafa, F., Enokido, T. (eds.) Advanced Information Networking and Applications, pp. 200–213. Springer International Publishing, Cham (2020). https://doi.org/10.1007/978-3-030-15032-7_18
8. Hoffman, K., Zage, D., Nita-Rotaru, C.: A survey of attack and defense techniques for reputation systems. ACM Comput. Surv. **42**(1) (2009). https://doi.org/10.1145/1592451.1592452
9. Hossain, S.: How blockchain technology and self-sovereign identity enables the new normal of remote learning, training and working (2023). https://www.linkedin.com/pulse/how-blockchain-technology-self-sovereign-identity-enables-hossain-/, linkedIn
10. Josang, A.: Trust and reputation systems. In: Foundations of Security Analysis and Design IV, pp. 209–245. Springer Nature (2007). https://doi.org/10.1007/978-3-540-74810-6_8
11. Kang, M., Lemieux, V.: A decentralized identity-based blockchain solution for privacy-preserving licensing of individual-controlled data to prevent unauthorized secondary data usage. Ledger **6** (2021). https://doi.org/10.5195/ledger.2021.239
12. Khare, R., Rifkin, A.: Weaving a web of trust. World Wide Web J. **2**(5896), 77–112 (1997). https://doi.org/10.1126/science.1163357
13. Lim, S.Y., Musa, O.B., Al-Rimy, B.A.S., Almasri, A.: Trust models for blockchain-based self-sovereign identity management: A survey and research directions. In: Maleh, Y., Tawalbeh, L., Motahhir, S., Hafid, A.S. (eds.) Advances in Blockchain Technology for Cyber Physical Systems, pp. 277–302. Springer International Publishing, Cham (2022). https://doi.org/10.1007/978-3-030-93646-4_13
14. Schaub, A., Bazin, R., Hasan, O., Brunie, L.: A trustless privacy-preserving reputation system. In: Hoepman, J.H., Katzenbeisser, S. (eds.) ICT Systems Security and Privacy Protection, pp. 398–411. Springer International Publishing, Cham (2016). https://doi.org/10.1007/978-3-319-33630-5_27
15. Seckler, M., Heinz, S., Forde, S., Tuch, A.N., Opwis, K.: Trust and distrust on the web: user experiences and website characteristics. Comput. Hum. Behav. **45**, 39–50 (2015). https://doi.org/10.1016/j.chb.2014.11.064
16. Soltani, R., Nguyen, U.T., An, A.: A survey of self-sovereign identity ecosystem. Secur. Commun. Netw. **2021**(1), 8873429 (2021). https://doi.org/10.1155/2021/8873429
17. Soska, K., Kwon, A., Christin, N., Devadas, S.: Beaver: a decentralized anonymous marketplace with secure reputation (2016). https://eprint.iacr.org/2016/464
18. W3C: Verifiable credentials data model v1.1 (2023). https://www.w3.org/TR/vc-data-model/. Accessed 26 Feb 2023
19. Werkheiser, B.: Goerli vs. Sepolia Testnet comparison: which is better?. https://www.alchemy.com/overviews/goerli-vs-sepolia. Accessed 05 Nov 2023

A Comparative Analysis of User Behaviour in DeFi Applications

Dorottya Zelenyanszki[1(✉)], Zhé Hóu[1], Kamanashis Biswas[2], and Vallipuram Muthukkumarasamy[1]

[1] Griffith University, Queensland, Australia
dora.zelenyanszki@griffithuni.edu.au
[2] Australian Catholic University, Sydney, Australia

Abstract. The Decentralised Finance (DeFi) community is continuously being affected by various types of security incidents that are causing high levels of financial loss. There have been multiple tools proposed for security attack detection, however, these cannot be used for general audit in DeFi applications as they focus on specific attacks or areas. This work aims to present how behavioural clustering and analysis can be leveraged to present insights into common user and smart contract behaviour in DeFi applications. Preliminary results are presented for two commonly known applications, Sushiswap and Uniswap V3 that lay down the foundation for general DeFi security audit.

Keywords: blockchain · DeFi · user behaviour · transaction analysis

1 Introduction

Decentralised Finance (DeFi) is a financial ecosystem that enables users to perform financial activities in a trustless and borderless manner due to the underlying blockchain [10]. It can offer various types of services including lending and token exchange [1]. As a result of its benefits, DeFi applications became very popular which can be seen by the 77% increase in Total Value Locked (TVL), reaching $103 billion, as reported by DappRadar's 2023 industry report[1]. The potential financial profit also prompted interest from malicious actors. These actors leverage various types of open issues such as vulnerabilities related to smart contracts and design to perform several kinds of attacks. For example, sandwich attacks or Pump-and-Dump (P&D) scams [7]. This caused a significant financial loss in the DeFi community. According to Chainalysis (see Footnote 1), in 2022 $3.7 billion was stolen. In 2023, there was a decrease to $1.7 billion, but the number of individual hacking incidents grew and the malicious actors became more sophisticated and diverse. As a result, the research community has an ongoing interest in providing tools for transaction audit and security protection. For example, leveraging symbolic execution, fuzzing and formal verification to detect smart contract vulnerabilities [4].

[1] https://www.chainalysis.com/blog/crypto-hacking-stolen-funds-2024/.

S. Kanhere et al. (Eds.): SDLT 2024, CCIS 2453, pp. 71–84, 2025.
https://doi.org/10.1007/978-981-96-4442-1_5

Interest in blockchain transaction analysis also increased as it can be utilised for various types of purposes including cryptocurrency market analysis [15], NFT community detection [3] and blockchain forensics [17] where the latter focuses on identifying malicious transactions and the corresponding adversarial actors. It can also be utilised to describe the users' behaviour in decentralised applications (dApps) such as classifying Ethereum users based on past behaviour [2]. The extraction of behavioural information can be useful in the analysis of security-related incidents as well as deducing the participants' habits and social interactions can be leveraged to determine their future actions including potentially malicious activities.

Previous research generally only focused on specific attacks such as sandwich attacks [6] or token leaking vulnerabilities [11] when it comes to security analyses and did not consider establishing general behavioural clusters for both normal and abnormal behaviour. General behavioural analysis can potentially present general adversarial behaviour that is present across various types of applications as the habits and interactions of the malicious actors can be extracted and analysed. For example, actors who usually act together can be revealed if their extracted behaviour is highly similar. It can be also utilised to analyse the long-term behaviour of addresses which can present if they have had a tendency to perform malicious activities in the past or if they are often prone to fall for certain types of scams. Appropriate actions can be taken by the developers of the applications to prevent malicious actors from having access to the application and users who are common victims can be notified of suspicious activities. It can be leveraged to detect DeFi attacks that happened in the past as well. These attacks can be linked to the involved addresses that can help the developers and authorities in their investigations. Behavioural analysis overall can introduce long-term patterns that can be utilised for detection, similarly how malicious transaction patterns and behavioural patterns can be leveraged for blockchain forensics purposes [13]. This work aims to present a comparison of the extractable general behaviour of two well-known DeFi applications, Sushiswap and Uniswap V3 with a reported trading volume of $6,411,043 and $1,111,949,320 according to CoinGecko[2]. The results for both were analysed based on selected features.

For this purpose, transaction data from a certain period was collected for both applications and the emitted transaction events were analysed to introduce general DeFi actions that can describe the users' past activities. These were utilised in an unsupervised clustering process which resulted in general behavioural clusters of the user and smart contract addresses involved in the DeFi applications. The clusters were analysed and preliminary results for behaviour that is present in the applications were described.

Contributions of this paper are listed as follows:

- Formation of general DeFi actions that can describe past user behaviour in DeFi application.

[2] https://www.coingecko.com/.

- General behavioural clusters that group addresses that correspond to similar behaviour that can be utilised to deduce adversarial actors' habits, connections and interactions.
- Comparison of two DeFi applications that was performed based on the behavioural cluster results.

The rest of the paper is structured as follows: Sect. 2 presents related research works that present the current DeFi scope and also describe current research tools for vulnerability and attack detection. Following that, in Sect. 3 the comparison of the two DeFi applications is presented regarding extractable user behaviour including the data collection, action formation, clustering and analysis steps. Finally, the paper is concluded in Sect. 4 where future directions are also mentioned.

2 Related Works

This section presents the current state of the DeFi landscape concerning security-related incidents and it also presents various types of research works that propose tools to detect vulnerabilities and attacks. These works, similarly to this research, aim to propose solutions that can be utilised for security audit and protection.

Liu et al. [8] presented the need to research DeFi users' perceptions as current research is limited to specific attacks or smart contract vulnerabilities. The authors conducted a semi-structured interview with DeFi users and an online survey afterwards. They aimed to research users' security risk awareness, the adequacy of employed security practices, how victims respond to DeFi attacks and how they mitigate these risks. They identified profitability and decentralisation as the main reasons users would use DeFi services. They also added that some of these users often blindly believe in decentralisation. Furthermore, they deduced that users do not apply adequate security controls and are overconfident in the use of two-factor authentication (2FA). Surprisingly, they also discovered that prior accident experience does not change users' perceptions as financial motivation overthrows their concerns, and even experience and education seem to be insufficient in increasing security levels. A large number of the users also do not support introduced regulations because of the potential additional fees which further presents the importance of profit as a major motivator in using DeFi services. They declared that the users' overall behaviour resembles gambling, therefore, the DeFi sector needs a similar type of regulatory system to the one implemented in the traditional gambling industry. They recommended that the community has to collectible work on regulation and also mentioned that DAO can be a potential tool as it can provide membership certificates to verified DeFi services. They also endorsed education and the use of regular reminders as tools that can improve users' security control. For example, a reminder feature that prompts users to review their token approvals.

Wang et al. [14] presented a mixed-method study to quantify the impact of sandwich attacks and show the knowledge gap between user perception and the actual effect of these attacks. Their results showed that miners started actively participating with attackers in relay services and also presented that attackers always achieve maximum profit. In general, they deduced that sandwich attacks achieved an increased influence on DeFi users.

Green et al. [5] proposed a DeFi survival analysis approach to describe user behaviour in lending protocols. Survival analysis uses time-to-event data and has been previously applied to Centralised Finance (CeFi) however, it was stated that its application to DeFi is not straightforward. They focused on seven transaction types: deposits, redeems, borrows, repays, liquidations, interest-rate swaps and reserve collateral usage toggling. These transactions always have one specific coin involved which they categorised into stablecoins and non-stablecoins. They utilised Kaplan-Meier curves for visualisation and when it was also required to show how the variables affect time to the outcome event, Cox regression was used. They used the analysis to deduce the subsequent transaction after the index event transaction. This is almost extensively the deposit transaction as before depositing any currency into an account, there are no other possible actions a user can take. They also utilised the analysis to check how long it takes for borrows to be repaid or liquidated and whether the type of the coin influences liquidations.

Wu et al. [16] presented that existing detection tools cannot detect based on logic as that would require an understanding of DeFi semantics. Their work concentrated on two common price manipulation attacks: the first presents when an attacker forces a DeFi app to perform an unwanted trade inside a DEX pool by finding and exploiting a vulnerability in the dApp and the second refers to attacks when an attacker manipulates the price of the token by exploiting the vulnerable DeFi app's price mechanism that depends on real-time status as the attacker can manipulate said status by trading in the pool. They aimed to detect these attacks by the analysis of invocations between smart contracts and high-level DeFi semantics. However, they identified that there is a gap between raw transactions and high-level semantics. They, therefore, defined semantics for three basic DeFi actions (such as transfer, minting and burning) and five advanced DeFi actions (such as trade, depositing and withdrawal). The basics were identified from the raw transactions and the advanced ones all consist of basic actions. To form these, they collected raw transactions and constructed Cash Flow Trees (CFTs) from them. These include contract invocations, events and basic actions. By applying three operations, connection, insertion and combination, they were able to lift the trees' semantics to advanced actions. They also pre-defined and utilised patterns to detect the attacks. For evaluation, they implemented a prototype system called DeFiRanger which identified four root causes of the price manipulation attacks: access control, design compatibility, slippage check and price dependency.

Su et al. [11] focused on weaknesses that originate from functional bugs such as token leaking vulnerabilities. They proposed a tool called DeFiWarder that traces transactions and provides protection from token-leaking vulnerabilities. Their solution also constructs CFTs and based on those it tracks the handlers of calls and mines the roles of the related addresses which then enables the capture of the real relationship between users and the accurate token flows of the users and the DeFi apps. It also merges the flows of different types of tokens, calculates the corresponding return rates and utilises abnormal cases to reveal token-leaking vulnerabilities. They identified arithmetic weakness, access control, control-flow hijacks, improper token transfer and price manipulation as causes of token leaking-related issues.

The related literature presented the effect and deep impact of DeFi security incidents and that the user adoption lacks accurate precision and security practice. It showed that the users are not educated on appropriate protection techniques and they are also generally against additional regulations. However, the high number of DeFi security incidents presents the need for tools that can provide security audits by the detection of adversarial activities. Related literature presented multiple types of DeFi security tools that were proposed for this purpose. However, these proposals have some limitations that this work's behavioural clusters aim to address. For example, they do not always take all transaction and event types into account as general behaviour is not their focus. They only consider one specific attack type such as price manipulation or sandwich attacks and some of them only show limited results as survival analysis only presents the potential next step after a certain index transaction. They rely on certain standards (for example ERC20), pre-defined rules, thresholds and the use of the flows of financial funds to make deductions regarding malicious intent. Other types of information coming from various types of events can present additional insights into the behaviour of DeFi users. General behavioural clusters can incorporate that to provide a general audit that focuses on a broader scope of DeFi and is not limited to a specific set of security attacks.

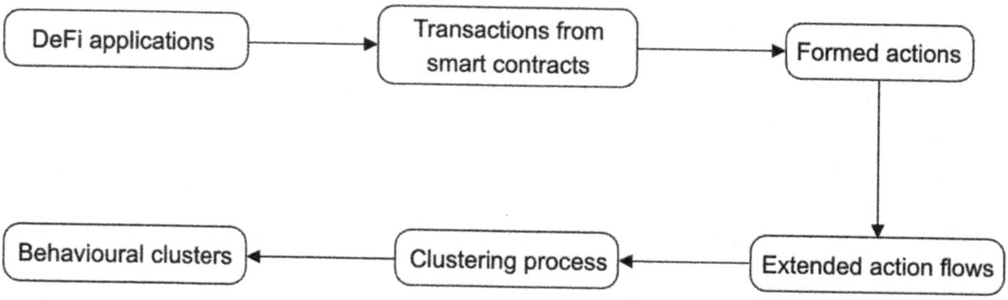

Fig. 1. Process to extract behavioural information.

3 User Behaviour in DeFi

This section presents the extraction of user behaviour from the examined two DeFi applications. At first, it is explained how transaction data is collected from the related smart contracts. Following that, the way the actions are formed and utilised to present the activities of the addresses in the form of action flows is also described. Subsequently, the clustering process is presented and then finally, the resulting behavioural clusters are described by calculated features. The overall process to extract behavioural information is presented in Fig. 1.

Table 1. Properties of the action nodes.

Property	Description
Total count	total # times action is called
Min call	min # times action is called
Max call	max # times action is called
Mean call	avg # times action is called
Min timestamp	first time action is called
Max timestamp	last time action is called

3.1 Data Collection and Action Formation

For the applications, transactions from smart contracts that are currently deployed[3][4] on Ethereum were collected that correspond to the period covered by block numbers 19993250 and 20207948. The Etherscan[5] and Alchemy[6] APIs were utilised to extract the transactions and decode the emitted events. The collected data then were added to a local Neo4j database so it could be queried to extract the necessary information to form actions and extract action flows. These flows present that in which order what kind of actions were performed by the corresponding address. The establishment of the local database followed the steps detailed in our previous work [18].

By querying the database, each included wallet addresses were extracted and categorised as whether they were smart contract or user-related. For Sushiswap 556 smart contract and 1800 user addresses were found, whereas for Uniswap V3 the ratio is 1211 smart contract and 2459 user addresses. However, not all of them actually initiated transactions within the examined period. By differentiating them and utilising behavioural clustering, both user and smart contract behaviour can be analysed separately. Apart from the wallet addresses, all token-related addresses were extracted as well.

Following this, the events that were emitted in transactions associated with these addresses were also retrieved. Every new unique set of events in transactions was added as a new DeFi action that can be performed by a wallet address.

[3] https://docs.sushi.com/docs/Developers/Deployment%20Addresses.
[4] https://docs.uniswap.org/contracts/v3/reference/deployments/ethereum-deployments.
[5] https://docs.etherscan.io/.
[6] https://docs.alchemy.com/reference/api-overview.

This is a simplified action formation process as further analysis of DeFi semantics is needed to introduce more defined actions. Overall, 89 actions were added for Sushiswap and 128 of them were formed for Uniswap. Among these actions, 21 of them were present in both applications. Since all transactions per address can be extracted from the local database, they were also all added as an action step made by either a user or a smart contract address. Each step consists of the action ID, wallet address, whether the address is a contract and the corresponding timestamp. The same was also performed for token addresses as well, however, in this case, the step only includes the action ID, token address and timestamp.

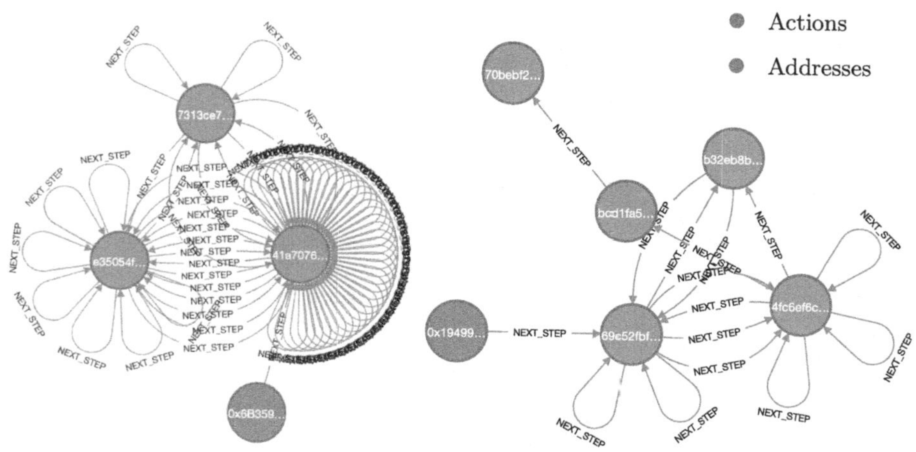

(a) Smart contract action flow (b) User action flow

Fig. 2. Action flows in Sushiswap.

After this, a second local database was established that includes three types of nodes: Address, token and action. For the action nodes numeric features were calculated that can be seen in Table 1. The address nodes have the wallet address and a boolean value that presents whether the address is a contract as properties. The token nodes have the token address and a boolean value that represents whether the token was used in multiple actions as property values. Two relationships were introduced between the nodes: i) NEXT_STEP which presents an action step performed by an address at a specific timestamp and it also covers the order of this step in the entire action flow that corresponds to that address; ii) USED_BY which represents the relation between an action and token that shows that this token was utilised in an action step that corresponds to that particular action. By filtering the NEXT_STEP relations through the address property, the corresponding action flows can be extracted. Through filtering, action flows for both user and contract addresses can be visualised. Figure 2 presents an example for both user and contract address action flows in Sushiswap.

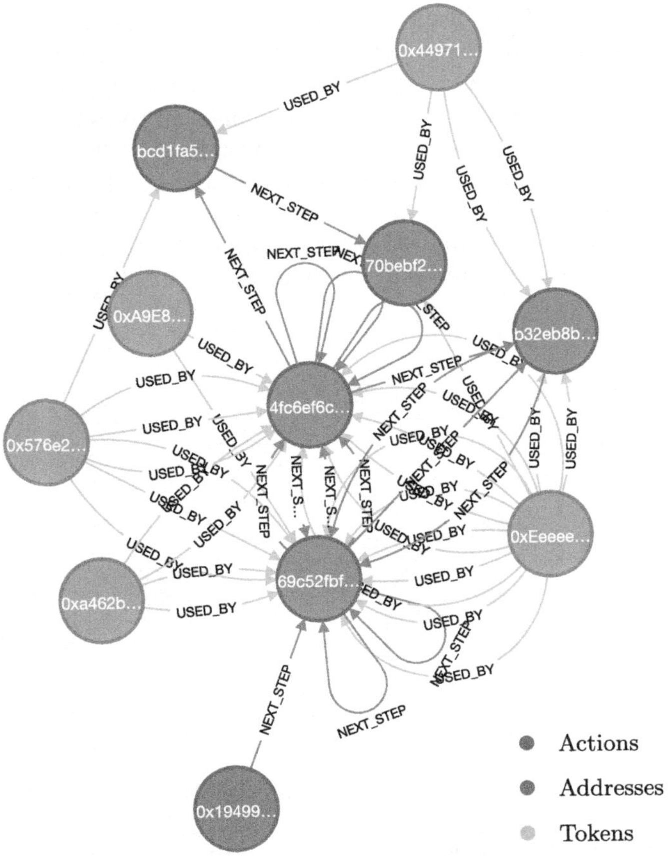

Fig. 3. An extended action flow.

3.2 Behavioural Clustering

As the token usage is also presented by the USED_BY relations, the action flows were extended by all USED_BY relations that had the particular address as a relation property. This way an action flow not only shows the order in which the actions performed but also present the kind of tokens the address interacted with. An example can be seen for this in Fig. 3. These action flows were utilised as input for a GNN model that provided graph-level embedding for them. Each embedding was added to two separate lists of embedding, one for the user and another for the smart-contract-related addresses. By separating them, user and smart contract behaviour can be examined separately. As there were no predefined labels that could be leveraged for the clustering process, the elbow method [12] was utilised to determine the required number of clusters for all four lists of embedding. The results for that are presented in Fig. 4. Multiple elbow points were calculated that are visualised by red colour in the corresponding figures. There were no elbow points found for the contract addresses in Uniswap as presented in Fig. 4c. This is the result of the fact that among many addresses extracted from event data, only a few of them initiated transactions within the examined period. As a result of this, the Uniswap contracts were excluded from the clustering. For the rest of them, the first identified elbow point was chosen as the value for the required number of clusters. However, for the Suhiswap contracts the addresses were only clustered into four clusters which probably is the result of the lower number of used contract addresses as well.

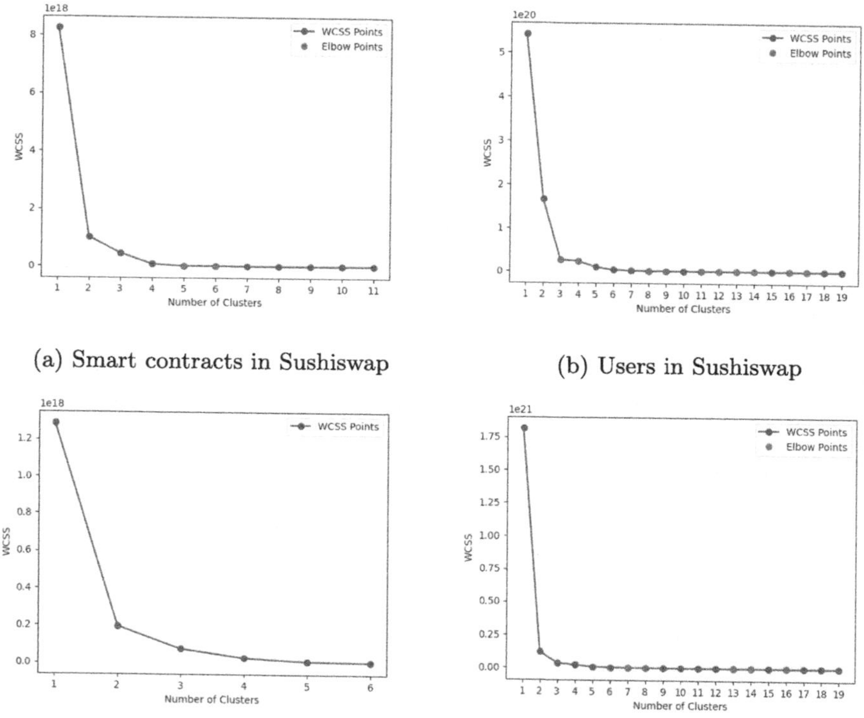

(a) Smart contracts in Sushiswap (b) Users in Sushiswap

(c) Smart contracts in Uniswap (d) Users in Uniswap

Fig. 4. Results of the elbow method.

The k-means clustering [9] clustering algorithm was utilised to cluster addresses that performed similar types of activities into separate behavioural clusters that can be analysed later. We have to note that given the short period that was examined, many addresses only had one performed action which is not sufficient enough to determine their past behaviour, thereby, the results presented in this paper are only preliminary and further data collection is required to show behaviour on a wider scale. Figure 5 presents examples (Cluster C_0 for all of them) for the created clusters where all included addresses and their NEXT_STEP relations are being visualised.

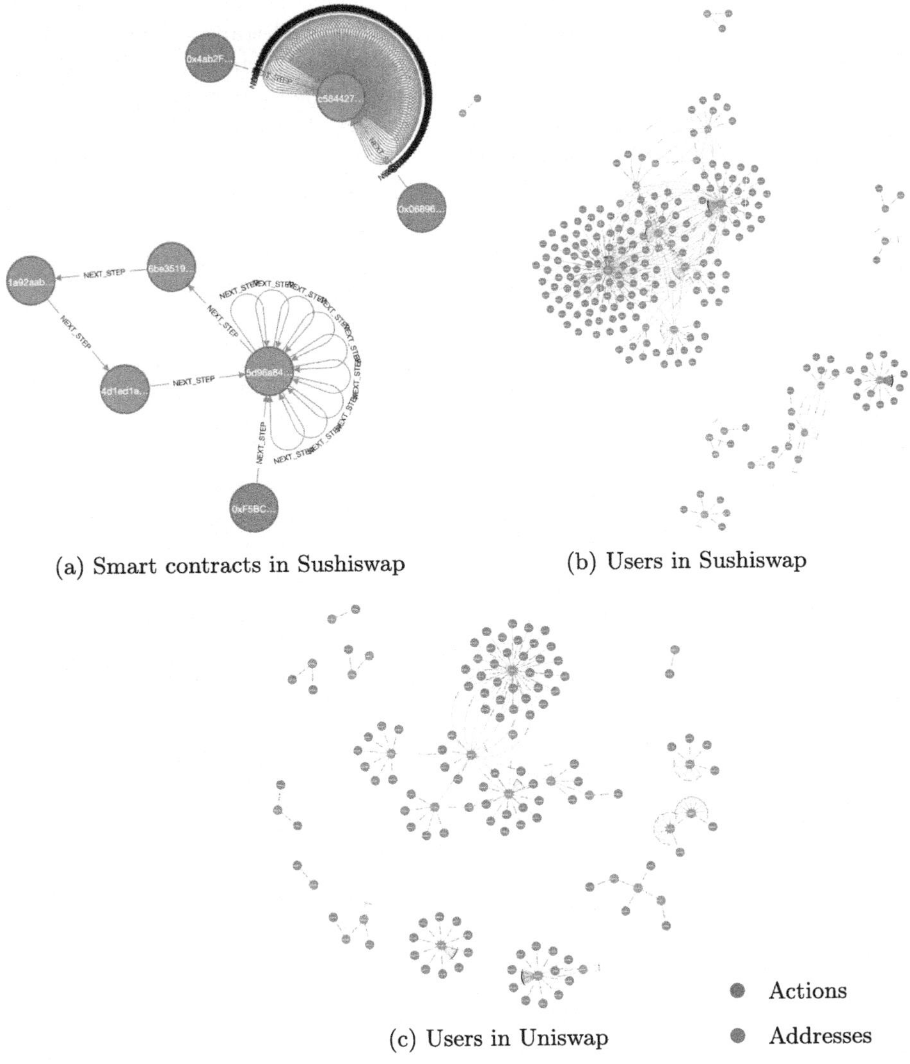

(a) Smart contracts in Sushiswap (b) Users in Sushiswap

(c) Users in Uniswap

Fig. 5. Cluster C_0 for all three embedding lists.

Table 2. Clusters for Sushiswap contracts.

#	Number of addresses	Number of actions	General action flow length	Number of unique tokens	Time (hr)
0	5	8	9	179	351.85
1	2	7	7	212	452.81
2	1	8	9	66	500.64
3	4	31	32	311	246.79

For the resulting behavioural clusters, multiple features were calculated as presented in Table 2, 3 and 4. The columns are explained: The number of addresses presents the addresses that belong to the particular cluster. The highest count action shows which action was performed the most by the addresses within that cluster. The number of actions highlights how many unique actions are performed in general by the included addresses, whereas the general action flow length presents how many actions were performed by them overall on average. The latter is based on a constructed general action flow which presents that at each possible action step which action will be performed most likely. The number of unique tokens shows how many unique tokens were included in the activities of each cluster and the highest count token presents which one was used the most. Time presents that on average how much time the addresses spent in the DeFi application within the examined period. It is presented in seconds. The highest count action and token columns were excluded from the Sushiswap tables as they presented the same values (action: 4fc6ef6c-8e83-41c3-bb7e-d81fbf184df4, token: 0xEeeeeEeeeEeEeeEeEeeEEEeeeeEeeeeeeeEEeE) for all clusters.

Table 3. Clusters for Sushiswap users.

#	Number of addresses	Number of actions	General action flow length	Number of unique tokens	Time (hr)
0	225	8	9	179	351.85
1	384	7	7	212	452.81
2	72	8	9	66	500.64

Table 4. Clusters for Uniswap users.

#	Number of addresses	Highest count action	Number of actions	General action flow length	Number of unique tokens	Highest count token	Time (hr)
0	407	b15b12be...	5	5	90	0x365Ac...	25.49
1	274	12b31f16...	4	4	102	0x365Ac...	1.17
2	44	12b31f16...	3	3	22	0x382ea...	3.48
3	19	12b31f16...	2	2	7	0x9e204...	0.07
4	55	4366058d...	6	6	52	0xD533a...	515.29
5	36	4693b2d2...	3	4	13	0x4e3FB...	509.90

3.3 Discussion

Based on the calculated features, preliminary behavioural information can be deduced for the addresses involved in these applications. In this section, we describe these results for both applications and also present some comparisons between them.

Sushiswap. For this application, the created clusters for the contract and user addresses are basically the same. This can be a consequence of the lower number of used addresses that can be leveraged in the clustering process but can also show that there is a connection between the behaviour of user and contract addresses. It is generally also shown that even though the addresses' behaviour is separated as that is clearly shown in the differing general action flows, they still have similarities as the most popular actions and tokens are the same across all clusters.

Uniswap. In this case, the clusters present very separate behaviours as the popular actions and tokens differ. However, the general action flows have many similarities as almost all of them start with the same action and some of them even have the first two action steps as the same. Information regarding users' activity levels can be also extracted. For example, users of Cluster C_4 can be generally viewed as active as they spent the longest time in the application within the examined period and performed the most actions on average, whereas Cluster C_3 can be described as inactive as the results present the opposite of Cluster C_4.

Comparison of the Two DeFi Applications. As the smart contract addresses could only be clustered for Sushiswap, the comparison was only conducted on the user-related addresses. It can be generally said that the users in Sushiswap were more active as they spent more time performing a higher variety of actions that utilised more unique tokens. However, in Uniswap the users' behaviour varies more. It was also deduced that although there are commonly formed actions that are present in both applications, only one of them was present in the most popular actions performed by the users in the clusters. This means that the activities available are similar types of DeFi services but they also differ which suggests that DeFi applications have their unique characteristics.

As the collected data only covers a short time period, these preliminary behavioural results cannot be considered as long-term DeFi behaviour in the selected applications. Further data collection will present how often addresses perform similar types of activities that were presented in this section. The preliminary results are not definite, some of the addresses that are currently included may present false or insufficient results. As this is also a result of the small dataset, future data collection and the consequent behavioural clustering will be able to address it.

4 Conclusion

DeFi applications offer several types of services that are similar to traditional banking which resulted in a high volume of funds associated with them. This also prompted the interest of scammers and hackers who exploit vulnerabilities in DeFi applications to gain financial profit. As the participating users' security practice adaption is lacking, various types of tools have been introduced that can be utilised for a security audit. However, these focus on specific attacks and they do not consider all information that can be extracted from transactions.

This work presents preliminary results of general behavioural clustering of addresses involved in DeFi applications. Similar behavioural analysis can be utilised to provide a general audit for DeFi applications. In this work transactions from two applications were extracted that cover a short period. The results presented separate address behaviour, however, the small dataset consisting of these transactions cannot be utilised to present long-term address behaviour. Therefore, in the future, a larger dataset will have to be leveraged to perform behavioural clustering that presents more comprehensive descriptions for the involved addresses. This can address current insufficient results like the lack of analysis of smart contract behaviour for Uniswap V3. At this stage, only two DeFi applications were utilised for behavioural clustering, however, other applications also have to be considered to present behaviour that is consistently present across DeFi. Behavioural analysis on an extended dataset can introduce emerging behavioural patterns that can be utilised in machine learning techniques to classify and predict DeFi-related security attacks and eventually be utilised in real-time analysis. Apart from that, DeFi semantics have to be analysed to form realistic actions as the current actions were added through a simplified process.

References

1. Amler, H., Eckey, L., Faust, S., Kaiser, M., Sandner, P., Schlosser, B.: DeFi-ning DeFi: challenges & pathway. In: 2021 3rd Conference on Blockchain Research & Applications for Innovative Networks and Services (BRAINS), pp. 181–184 (2021). https://doi.org/10.1109/BRAINS52497.2021.9569795
2. Bonifazi, G., Corradini, E., Ursino, D., Virgili, L.: Defining user spectra to classify ethereum users based on their behavior. J. Big Data **9** (2022). https://doi.org/10.1186/s40537-022-00586-3
3. Casale-Brunet, S., Ribeca, P., Doyle, P., Mattavelli, M.: Networks of ethereum non-fungible tokens: A graph-based analysis of the ERC-721 ecosystem. In: 2021 IEEE International Conference on Blockchain (Blockchain), pp. 188–195. IEEE Computer Society, Los Alamitos, CA, USA (2021). https://doi.org/10.1109/Blockchain53845.2021.00033, https://doi.ieeecomputersociety.org/10.1109/Blockchain53845.2021.00033
4. Chu, H., Zhang, P., Dong, H., Xiao, Y., Ji, S., Li, W.: A survey on smart contract vulnerabilities: data sources, detection and repair. Inf. Softw. Technol. **159**, 107221 (2023)
5. Green, A., Cammilleri, C., Erickson, J.S., Seneviratne, O., Bennett, K.P.: Defi survival analysis: Insights into risks and user behaviors. In: Pardalos, P., Kotsireas, I., Guo, Y., Knottenbelt, W. (eds.) Mathematical Research for Blockchain Economy, pp. 127–141. Springer International Publishing, Cham (2023). https://doi.org/10.1007/978-3-031-18679-0_8
6. Heimbach, L., Wattenhofer, R.: Eliminating sandwich attacks with the help of game theory. In: Proceedings of the 2022 ACM on Asia Conference on Computer and Communications Security, pp. 153–167. ASIA CCS 2022, Association for Computing Machinery, New York, NY, USA (2022). https://doi.org/10.1145/3488932.3517390

7. Li, W., Bu, J., Li, X., Peng, H., Niu, Y., Zhang, Y.: A survey of DeFi security: challenges and opportunities. J. King Saud Univ. Comput. Inf. Sci. **34**(10), 10378–10404 (2022)
8. Liu, M., et al.: I experienced more than 10 DeFi scams: on DeFi users' perception of security breaches and countermeasures (2024). https://arxiv.org/abs/2406.15709
9. MacQueen, J.: Some methods for classification and analysis of multivariate observations. In: Proceedings of the Fifth Berkeley Symposium on Mathematical Statistics and Probability, vol. 1, pp. 281–297. Oakland, CA, USA (1967)
10. Meyer, E., Welpe, I.M., Sandner, P.G.: Decentralized finance—a systematic literature review and research directions. ECIS (2022)
11. Su, J., et al.: Defiwarder: Protecting defi apps from token leaking vulnerabilities. In: 2023 38th IEEE/ACM International Conference on Automated Software Engineering (ASE), pp. 1664–1675 (2023). https://doi.org/10.1109/ASE56229.2023.00110
12. Thorndike, R.L.: Who belongs in the family? Psychometrika **18**(4), 267–276 (1953)
13. Ul Hassan, M., Rehmani, M.H., Chen, J.: Anomaly detection in blockchain networks: a comprehensive survey. IEEE Commun. Surv. Tutorials **25**(1), 289–318 (2023). https://doi.org/10.1109/COMST.2022.3205643
14. Wang, Y., Zuest, P., Yao, Y., Lu, Z., Wattenhofer, R.: Impact and user perception of sandwich attacks in the DeFi ecosystem. In: Proceedings of the 2022 CHI Conference on Human Factors in Computing Systems. CHI 2022, Association for Computing Machinery, New York, NY, USA (2022). https://doi.org/10.1145/3491102.3517585
15. Wu, J., Liu, J., Zhao, Y., Zheng, Z.: Analysis of cryptocurrency transactions from a network perspective: an overview. J. Netw. Comput. Appl. **190**, 103139 (2021)
16. Wu, S., et al.: DeFiRanger: Detecting DeFi price manipulation attacks. IEEE Trans. Dependable Secure Comput. **21**(4), 4147–4161 (2024). https://doi.org/10.1109/TDSC.2023.3346888
17. Wu, Y., et al.: A bitcoin transaction network analytic method for future blockchain forensic investigation. IEEE Trans. Netw. Sci. Eng. **8**(2), 1230–1241 (2021). https://doi.org/10.1109/TNSE.2020.2970113
18. Zelenyanszki, D., Hóu, Z., Biswas, K., Muthukkumarasamy, V.: Linking nft transaction events to identify privacy risks. In: International Symposium on Distributed Ledger Technology, pp. 82–97. Springer (2023). https://doi.org/10.1007/978-981-97-0006-6_6

Incentivising Decentralisation with Harberger Tax

Hans Song, Naipeng Dong(✉), and Guangdong Bai

The University of Queensland, St. Lucia, Brisbane, QLD, Australia
h.song@uq.net.au, {n.dong,g.bai}@uq.edu.au

Abstract. Proof of Work blockchains are write-only ledgers existing on peer to peer networks, requiring new data to go through a computationally expensive validation process by *miners* who dedicate their hardware in return for financial compensation. While a core principle of blockchains is to be decentralised, the vast majority of miners choose to form coalitions and pool their computational power, negating the decentralised nature of the blockchain. In this paper, the concept of computation was gamified through an economic model with a focus on incentivising the distribution computational power through the application of Harberger Tax and auction mechanisms is proposed and formalised. A state generator was created based on a simplified deterministic version of the model to formalise potential strategies, observe expected behaviour, and make predictions of expected rewards based on participant strategies. A simulation was then created to validate the predictions against a more realistic implementation of the model. These tools revealed that while there are some flaws in the model, it has potential to incentivise the distribution of computational power. Finally, further areas of investigation have been identified for future research.

Keywords: Blockchain · Decentralisation · Incentive · Harberger Tax

1 Introduction

At it's core, blockchain is about creating a public ledger that ensures immutability through decentralisation. While there have been many implementations, all platforms require overcoming the issue of reaching consensus in a distributed trust-less environment. Bitcoin [12] is the platform which spurred the demand for innovation in blockchains with Satoshi Nakamoto's innovative Proof of Work (PoW) consensus algorithm. Bitcoin now stands at the forefront of cryptocurrencies with market capitalisation fluctuating around 100 billion USD [2], utilising an estimated 55TWh annually [5] as of November 2020.

The security of the PoW consensus algorithm (refer to Sect. 2.1) is established through computationally expensive cryptographic puzzles to prove the "work" contributed to the validation of a block. These are solved by *miners*, people or companies that dedicate computational power to guess the solution for a

S. Kanhere et al. (Eds.): SDLT 2024, CCIS 2453, pp. 85–102, 2025.
https://doi.org/10.1007/978-981-96-4442-1_6

reward. Dedicating more resources gives miners a higher probability of guessing the solution. As blockchains utilising PoW rose in popularity, the number of competing miners seeking to profit from the rewards rose alongside. While there are still individual miners, the bulk of computation stems from miners that have contributed their computational power to a *pool*, a congregation of miners lead by a pool supervisor who coordinates work and distributes rewards. Amortised, this would result in similar payouts to mining individually, with smaller payout and increased frequency, resulting in reduced variance. However, this also leads to large portions of computational power aggregated under the authority of singular entities, effectively centralising computation.

With four pools contributing almost 60% of the total hash rate for Bitcoin [1] at the time of this writing and a real possibility for pools to exceeded 50% (such as GHash [4] in 2014). The only limiting factor is the pools goodwill, potential public backlash and a shared incentive to maintain the reputation and valuation of the currency. As each pool has a centralised authority orchestrating operations, the scenario in which they collude to execute a 51% attack is a possibility. Additionally, pool supervisors are able to censor transactions by excluding them from the blocks they mine. This trend and it's potential effects has been investigated previously to through varying methods [8,9].

This project introduces and verifies an economic model inspired by the Harberger Tax (refer to Sect. 2.4) that has a focus on encouraging the separation the authority from pool supervisors to external participants, negating the vulnerability introduced by the centralisation of authority. This is achieved by creating a sharing economy (refer to Sect. 2.5) in which individual miners or pools can offer their computational power to a public marketplace as *chunks* from which external participants or other miners may purchase to become *owners*. Through this marketplace, miners will be consistently rewarded with taxation on their contributed power while owners can have a chance at the block reward without the hardware or power required. Additionally, this means that pools no longer need to adhere to the rule of having less than 50% of the global hash rate as the authority is in the hands of the owners. The aim of the model is to attract pools to utilise the model as contributors (*miners*) rather than participants (*owners*). In order to verify the economic model, it will first be formally defined and modelled with a deterministic state generator. Then, a simulation implementing the model will be created in order to optimise parameters and to observe any potential predisposed trends. Using the optimal parameters, the model's performance can be assessed through the actions of the participants as they make decisions purchasing chunks within the simulation.

2 Background and Related Work

2.1 Proof of Work (PoW) Consensus

Consensus algorithms are at the core of any blockchain and are an attempt at overcoming the issue of overall system consistency despite faulty or malicious participants in a distributed, trust-less environment. As a distributed system, data sent over the network is never guaranteed to reach their destination and can be intercepted by malicious actors. Hence, a strategy is required to both ensure the integrity of the chain, and ensure that the correct version is received by as many participants as possible.

PoW overcomes the aforementioned issue using a variation of HashCash [6] by creating a cryptographic puzzle with merkle trees that is computationally expensive with the solution used as verification for the next block. Attempting to rewrite history or faking blocks requires having enough computational power to solve the puzzles of each related block and overtake the creation of the next block, creating a chain that is longer than the honest chain.

2.2 Mining

Each block on a blockchain contains a timestamp, verified transactions, and most importantly a cryptographic hash of the previous block which facilitates the chaining. The process of mining a block is designed to be prohibitively difficult and aims to be solvable in a consistent time. It involves several components:

- T - A collection of unverified transactions (not yet on the blockchain)
- t - The digest of a merkle tree created from T
- h_p - The hash of the previous block.
- n - A random string otherwise known as the *nonce*.
- λ - The difficulty of the puzzle (where $\lambda > 1$) where λ is the required number of zeroes padding the solution (changes every 2016 blocks).
- $\mathcal{H}$ - The hash function chosen by the miner that outputs 256 bits based on the input.
- H - Hash rate of the miner, the number of times $\mathbb{H}$ can be executed per second.

The miner is required to verify transactions T and *pack* them by hashing them into a merkle tree. Then, they must create a suitable hash for the block. A potential hash is found via the function $h = \mathcal{H}(t\|h_p\|n)$ with each attempt changing n (and occasionally t). When an appropriate nonce is chosen, h should satisfy the condition $h \leq \frac{2^{256}}{\lambda}$ to be a suitable solution. The difficulty λ is chosen such that the computational work necessary to solve the problem will require the full block time. That is, when the total hash rate of the miners increase, the difficulty also increases to keep the mining time constant. As the difficulty keep increasing over these years, it has been known that it is not profitable to mine with general computers. Therefore, mining pools are invented to gather minor's computational power together for better rewards.

2.3 Mining Pools

While the intention of PoW is for each participant mine individually for a truly decentralised implementation, there is no punishment for collusion, nor is behaving honestly always the most profitable method of participation. Since most miners are incentivised by profit rather than maintaining the integrity of the blockchain they will seek to increase their hash rate for a better chance at the reward. However, as the global hash rate increases, the difficulty is adjusted to control block creation speed. In response to the increased difficulty, miners have formed coalitions to pool their resources. Both work and rewards are delegated to participants. While the amount would be very similar to mining individually, the variance of payout is reduced.

As of 1 Nov 2020, the hash rate distribution is seen in Fig. 1 below.

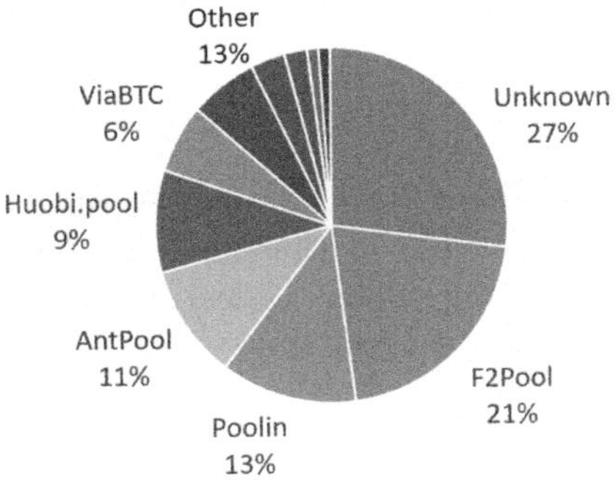

Fig. 1. Hash rate distribution over a 24 h period [3].

While a *sufficiently* distributed network means that the computational power of an entity should never exceed 50% or more of the global hash rate, a higher degree of fragmentation would be preferred for a securer network.

2.4 Harberger Tax

The Harberger Tax [14] is an economic policy that aims to prevent unequal distribution of property through two rules: 1) Owners assign a self-assessed value to their property and pay a proportional tax. 2) The owner is unable to prevent anybody from purchasing their property at their previously set price.

The purpose of the first rule is to discourage owners from monopolising their property by assigning a prohibitively high price to prevent others from purchasing as they themselves would have to shoulder the proportional tax. The next rule ensures the mobility of property and that there is no incentive to invest in their property as it is likely to be taken at any given point. This combats the issue of price inflation where an owner may "hold" their property and increase demand and inflate the price. It will also ensure owners do not set their price too low to avoid taxation.

2.5 Strategic Game

A model can be considered a strategic game if it consists of a finite set of decision-makers N from which each decision-maker has a non-empty set of action profiles

A_i that are non-revocable and will be executed simultaneously based on associated preferences [13, Section 2.1]. A key factor is that each decision-maker's preferences must also take into account all possible decisions in the game. This definition can be applied to a wide variety of scenarios including the economic model in this proposal, with participants acting as the decision-makers, and their actions being based on not only their own circumstances, but also the actions of other participants.

Nash Equilibrium is the proposed *steady state* in which all players are acting based on the *best decision* they can while aware of the actions their opponent(s) will take [13, Section 2.2]. Once the strategies of all players, the possible decisions, and all possible game states are defined (at least in natural language) according to the requirements of a strategic game, a Nash equilibrium exists for any action profile in which all players make a decision such that no player can make a decision that results in an outcome more preferred than the current game state. Determining the Nash equilibrium yields strategies to ensure participants are not incentivised to deviate from the expected behaviour and gain an unfair advantage.

2.6 Related Work

Two Phase PoW [7] introduces an additional puzzle that requires the use of a private key to sign the work done. While this method would discourage outsourcing, it essentially negates any possibility of public pools that miners rely on for reduced variance. P2Pool [16] is an attempt at creating a completely decentralised mining pool (i.e. without a supervisor) but it is riddled with technical issues, high overhead, and much higher variance compared to other pools. Smartpool [10] is another proposed solution in which the pool is orchestrated via a smart contract (a self-executing) on the Ethereum blockchain. This is a valid solution that may solve the centralisation of authority for public pools, however there is no incentive for private pools to utilise such a method. NiceHash and many other similar platforms, are cryptocurrency hash power brokers in which members can rent hashing power to contribute to a pool of their choice. They make no attempts to address the issue of authority centralisation, rather, their platform enables and encourages it.

3 System Overview and Its Economic Model

Our system requires the following entities: Any number of *miners* who contribute computational power; The *pool* that manages and allocates the dedicated computational power into *chunks*; The *orchestrator* that delegates work to participants, holds unowned chunks; Any number of *participants* (who may be miners) who purchase and sell the authority over the computational power through ownership of chunks.

For the purposes of this project, the orchestrator and pool act as a single entity (though an implementation could be based on any number of means such as a dedicated server or smart contract). The ownership of each chunk is taxed according to the Harberger tax (refer to Sect. 2.4), with some additions:

- When a participant wishes to purchase a chunk, an auction is initiated. During which, any other participant may chose to participate and bid for the chunk.
- When a participant is unable to afford the tax, they relinquish ownership of their chunk.
- Any unowned property is returned to a global pool of unowned property that participants may attempt to purchase through auction starting at the pools sale price.

Between each block validated, the orchestrator initiates the trade phase. During this phase, participants may initiate auctions and compete for the ownership of chunks. At the end of the trade phase, participants are taxed according to the number of chunks in their possession and their self-assessed valuation. This trade phase may occur multiple times between validated blocks or once per any number of validated blocks depending on the orchestrator. In the event the pool successfully validates a block, the reward is distributed according to the number of chunks in a participants possession.

3.1 The Economic Model

The economic model contains the following components to create an approximated strategic game.

Chunks. All computational power dedicated to the system will be divided on the basis of a predefined number of chunks to form arbitrary discrete units of computational power. While it is unknown whether or not computational power can be divided based on an arbitrary number for a practical implementation, the computational power represented by each chunk will be equal for the purposes of modelling the system.

Participants. The participants are individuals who may or may not have ownership of some amount of computational power but participate in the system in order to buy and sell chunks of computational power. A participant may be defined as: $\rho := (x, p_s, p_b, f(s))$, where

- x - Owned chunks - The number of chunks owned by the participant.
- p_s - **Price of sale** - The self-evaluated price set by the participant on their owned chunks.
- p_b - **Buying price** - The price at which the participant purchased a chunk during an auction.
- $f(s)$ - **Function mapping a state** to the participants decision.

During each interval, the participant may chose to initiate an auction given their balance is sufficient or to withhold and not take any action (refer to Sects. 4.1 to 4.1 for more details).

Pool. The pool acts as the conceptual host of the system, orchestrating auctions and rewarding participants relative to the block time. It is also responsible for managing the tax, dividing, and allocating chunks. A functional implementation would ideally be decentralised and deployed on a blockchain. A blockchain can be defined as: $P := (C, H, t, r, S_\rho)$ where $S_\rho = \{\rho_0, \rho_1, \ldots, \rho_n\}$.

- C - total **c**hunks - The total number of chunks to divide contributed computational power.
- r - Tax **r**ate - The amount retained by the pool prior to distributing the reward, proportional to the participants price and number of owned chunks.
- S_ρ - **S**et of participants - The participants contributing to this pool.

Blockchain. An imitation of a real-world blockchain. For the purposes of the model, the actual creation and validation of the block is considered a constant. The discount factor may be used to imitate the depreciation in value of the cryptocurrency. Each blockchain can be defined as: $B := (\mathbb{R}, \mathbb{H}, b, d, S_{po})$ where $S_{po} = \{P_0, P_1, \ldots, P_n\}$, with

- $\mathbb{R}$ - Block **r**eward - The value awarded on successfully validating a block of an arbitrary unit.
- $\mathbb{H}$ - Global **h**ash rate - The total computational power dedicated to the blockchain.
- b - **B**lock time - The interval on which a new block is created.
- d - **d**iscount factor - The rate at which the valuation of the blockchains currency depreciates over time.
- S_{po} - **S**et of **po**ols - The Pools contributing computational power to this blockchain.

Game. Containing all the components defined above, the game G is defined as:$G := (T_i, S_b)$ with $S_b = \{B_0, B_1, \ldots, B_n\}$, and

- T_i - **T**ime **i**nterval - Represents a discrete time interval $i \in [0 \rightarrow \infty)$, that dictates a change in the state at each observed increment
- S_b - **S**et of **B**lockchains - the blockchains that exist in the Universe of Discourse.

Relations among the Notations. The expected reward for the ownership of a chunk is $R = \frac{\mathbb{R}}{c} \times \frac{H}{\mathbb{H}}$. Reward per chunk with taxation and discount factor applied is $R(d) = R \times (1 - r) \times \left(\frac{1}{1+d}\right)^d$. The amount taxable is $t(x) = x \times p_s \times (1 - r)$. The instantaneous profit from a purchase is $p_{purchase} = (x + y) \times R - t(x) - t(y) - y \times p_b$. The instantaneous profit from withholding $p_{held} = x \times R - t(x)$. The instantaneous profit from a sale $p_{sale} = (y \times p_s)$.

At time T_0, all participants begin with $x = 0$ and a randomised amount of funds. Between each interval T_i to T_{i+1}, participants will have an opportunity to initiate an auction for any of the available chunks from the pool at a starting rate of p_p or from any of the other participants at their set price p_s while keeping in mind their potential profit from Sects. 3.1 to 3.1. A reward is distributed to chunk owners according to Sect. 3.1 or Sect. 3.1 depending on the discount factor. Finally, a tax is deducted from each participant according to Sect. 3.1 where $x = participant.x$ at T_{i+1}.

4 Design and Implementation

4.1 Deterministic State Generator

A custom modeller was created to generate the set of all possible states and transitions for querying paths and reachability. The state generator accepts the following as parameters as a basis to creating states: r - Tax rate, d - Discount factor, R - Expected reward per owned chunk, t - Threshold at which to consider the reward as too low.

For the purposes of modelling, each **participant** is represented by an object with the following properties:

- *balance* - the current value in the participants possession as a unit of the block reward.
- *chunks* - the current number of chunks in the participants possession.
- *chance* - A chance used to determine if a participant will participate, initiate an auction, or withhold.

Each **state** created in the state generator can be defined as:

$$S := (c, depth, action, P) \ with \ P = \{p_0, p_1, \ldots, p_n\}, \tag{1}$$

- c - The probability of reaching this state. Refer to Sect. 4.1 below.
- *depth* - The number of steps to reach this state (or depth).
- *action* - The action taken to transition to this state.
- P - A set of participant objects containing their initial state.

Each state represents the funds and chunks of each participant and maintains a reference to future states.

An **action** represents the decision made by one or many participants to change the current state or by the distribution of a reward. It may be represented as:

$$A := (\tau, c, S_t), \ with \ S_t = t_0, t_1, \ldots, t_n, \ and \ \tau \in \{\textsc{Reward}, \ \textsc{Purchase}\}, \tag{2}$$

- τ - The transition type.
- c - The probability of this transition occurring.
- S_t - The set of transactions executed in this transition. Zero or more discrete transactions such that $\forall t \in S_t : \nexists \, t' \in S_t : t.buyer = t'.buyer$.

A **transaction** contains details about the transferral of chunk ownership between participants and can be defined as the following:

$$T := (buyer, seller, price) \tag{3}$$

- *buyer* - The buyer who initiated the transaction.
- *seller* - The seller from which the chunk will be transferred from.
- *price* - The price at which the buyer is purchasing for.

Modelling. In order to facilitate the modelling of the game, the probability of a participants actions can be defined on set of participants P satisfying:

- $\forall b \in Buyers : b.chance > 0 \wedge b.funds \geq 1$
- $\forall s \in Sellers : b.chunks \geq 1$
- $P(b_{purchase}) = \frac{b.chance}{Sellers.length}$
- $f(s) = \begin{cases} P(b_{purchase}) & \text{if } b \text{ chooses to purchase} \\ P(1 - b_{purchase}) & \text{else if } b \text{ can purchase but chooses to withhold} \\ 1 & \text{else if } b \text{ has insufficient funds to purchase} \end{cases}$

The probability of reaching a state X may then be calculated as the product of actions taken to reach it:

$$P(X) = P(X_{prev}) \times \prod_{i=1}^{Buyers} action(b_i).$$

The expected reward may then be calculated using the product of the balances at each end state and the state probability. Given a set of end states $\{X_{x|0}, X_{x|1}, \ldots, X_{x|n}\}$, where $X_{x|i}$ represents the balance of participant x at the ith state X. Hence for participant x, the expected reward can be calculated as:

$$\mathbb{E}(R(x \mid i)) = \sum_{i=0}^{n} X_{x|i} \times P(X_{x|i}).$$

Algorithms. The following algorithms captures the logic in order to create a Deterministic State Generator according to the above game specifications.

Algorithm 1 shows the process for which states were recursively generated. A new state is created for each potential combination or subset of possible transactions the participants are able to take in the current state until no more actions can be taken or the reward is reduced below a threshold due to the discount factor. Algorithm 2 generates all possible combinations and subsets of transactions given the current participants state. It accepts the set of participants S_ρ as the basis for determining possible transactions. Algorithm 3 below determines the probability distribution of states belonging to a parent state. It considers all participants with the ability to purchase and determines the probability of each action occurring. Participants who are not in the set B defined in line 2 are considered to not be eligible for purchasing and are not considered as they would not have a choice. Algorithm 4 below updates the state of each participant to apply a transition to the state owning the given set of participants.

The source code for the implementation used for the purposes of this project can be found on Gitlab[1]. Created in TypeScript [11], it provides a command line interface with a number of options to programmatically change how the resultant states are generated.

In addition to the generator, a visualisation utility was added utilising Mermaid [15] which enabled rendering smaller scale state diagrams for visual inspection. A maximum depth of 30 yielded over 2.5 million states in 40 s and utilising

[1] https://gitlab.com/harberger-tax/state-diagram-generator.

Algorithm 1. Recursive state generator

```
procedure GENERATESTATES(S_ρ, state, depth)
    r ← R(depth)                                          ▷ refer to section 3.1
    if r < t then
        return
    end if
    state.subStates ← EMPTY SET OF STATE
    S_t ← GENERATETRANSACTIONS(S_ρ)                       ▷ refer to algorithm 2
    S_c ← CALCULATESTATECHANCE(state, S_t, S_ρ)           ▷ refer to algorithm 3
    for i ∈ [0, S_t.length) do
        action ← new ACTION(S_t[i], S_c[i])
        S'_ρ ← APPLYACTION(S_ρ, action)                   ▷ refer to algorithm 4
        subState ← new STATE(S'_ρ, action)
        state.subStates ← state.subStates ∪ {subState}
        GENERATESTATES(S'_ρ, subState, depth + 1)
    end for
end procedure
```

Algorithm 2. Transaction combination generator

```
procedure GENERATETRANSACTIONS(S_ρ)
    B ← {b ∈ S_ρ | b.balance ≥ 1 ∧ b.chance > 0}
    S ← {s ∈ S_ρ | s.chunks ≥ 1}
    transactionSets ← EMPTY SET OF SET OF TRANSACTION
    for b ∈ B do
        set ← EMPTY SET OF TRANSACTION
        for s ∈ S do
            set ← set ∪ {new TRANSACTION(b, s)}
        end for
        transactionSets ← transactionSets ∪ {set}
    end for
    result ← EMPTY SET OF SET OF TRANSACTION
    unvisited ← TransactionSets
    while unvisited ≠ ∅ do
        set ← unvisited.POP()
        for transaction ∈ set do
            for otherSet ∈ unvisited do
                for otherTransaction ∈ otherSet do
                    if transaction.seller ≠ otherTransaction.seller
                        ∨ transaction.seller.chunks > 1 then
                        result ← result ∪ {[transaction, otherTransaction]}
                    end if
                end for
            end for
            result ← result ∪ {[transaction]}
        end for
    end while
    return result
end procedure
```

over 5 GB of ram. At a discount factor of 0.01, a tax rate of 0.05, and a threshold of 0.009, the maximum depth required at 4713 would not be feasible as the amount of memory required to create the complete set states far exceed the computational resources available.

Figure 2 shows a small sample set of states generated with participants having a chance of 0.9 and a maximum depth of 1. Each node contains information on the current state of each participant in the form Pi: c, f where i is the ID of the participant, c is the owned chunks, and f is the current balance. Each arrow represents a transition in which either the distribution of chunks or funds of any participant observes a change and are labelled with the chance for the transition to occur and the reason for the transition (A purchase, reward, or no change occurred).

Algorithm 3. Determines the chance of a state given a transition and parent state.

```
procedure CALCULATESTATECHANCE(T, S_ρ)
    B ← {b ∈ S_ρ | b.balance ≥ 1 ∧ b.chance > 0}
    S ← {s ∈ S_ρ | s.chunks ≥ 1}
    chances ← 1
    for b ∈ B do
        if t ∈ T : t.buyer = b then
            chances ← chances × b.chance / length(S − b)
        else
            chances ← chances × (1 − b.chance)
        end if
    end for
    total ← 1
    return chances
end procedure
```

Algorithm 4. Applies a transition on a state

```
procedure APPLYACTION(S_ρ, a)
    switch a.τ do
        case REWARD
            for ρ ∈ S_ρ do
                ρ.funds ← ρ.funds + R(ρ.chunks)            ▷ refer to section 3.1
            end for
        case PURCHASE
            for t ∈ action.S_t do
                t.buyer.funds ← t.buyer.funds − t.price
                t.buyer.chunks ← t.buyer.chunks + 1
                t.seller.funds ← t.seller.funds + t.price
                t.seller.chunks ← t.seller.chunks − 1
            end for
end procedure
```

4.2 Simulation

The simulation aims to be as close a representation of a potential game run as possible. Unlike the Deterministic State Generator, the simulation maintains a single persistent state that is updated based on a semi-random process rather than generating possible states.

Algorithm 5 shows the looped execution of the simulation. The simulation iterates until the reward is reduced below a threshold. At each iteration, if the round matches up to the block interval, a reward may be distributed depending on a random number generated against the pool's global compute share. Algorithm 6 rolls a generates a random float in the interval [0, 1] against the pool's global compute share. If the roll was successful, the reward is distributed amongst the participants, with the leftover awarded to the pool. Algorithm 7 simulates the auction process for a standard open auction in which participants bid for the highest price. Algorithm 8 considers the participants current state, the current bid, and the participants strategy in order to determine if the participant should (or can) participate[2].

[2] The source code can be found on Gitlab[3].

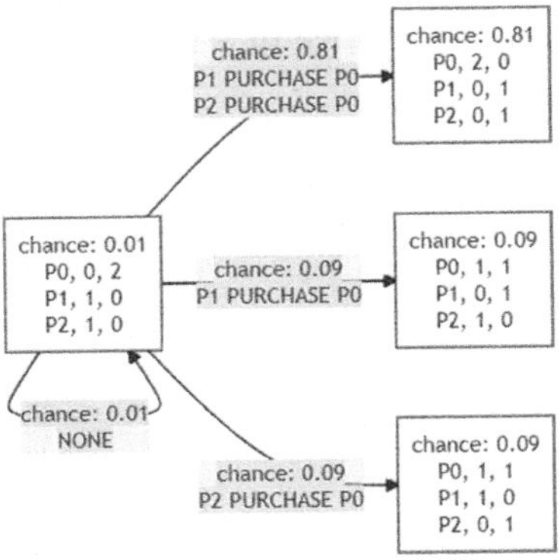

Fig. 2. Deterministic state generator minimal example

5 Results

5.1 Deterministic State Generator

As the hardware limitations prevent the creation of complete system models, a smaller subset was utilised for analysis. All systems were created with the following parameters (parameters were inflated to accelerate the decay of reward valuation): Block reward 1, Initial chunks 2, Initial funds 1, Initial chunks 0, Reward minimum threshold 0.009, maximum depth 15.

A test was run using the generator for participant probabilities ranging from 0.1 to 0.9 for both participants with a tax rate of 0 and 0.2 (the test script can be found in the repository). Only one participant is considered as they are symmetrical in all aspects.

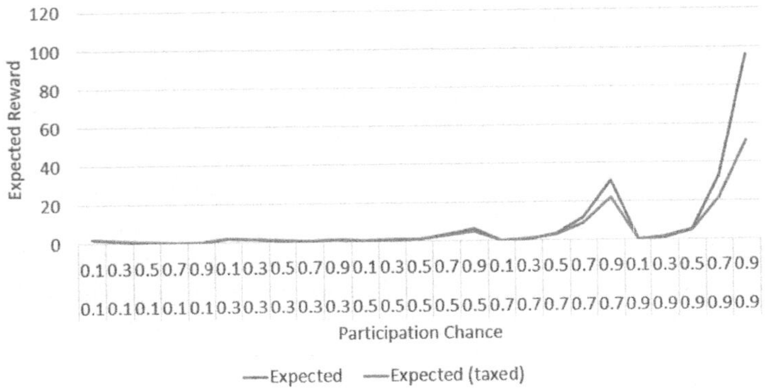

Fig. 3. Expected reward per combination of participant purchase probability

The results in Fig. 3 shows the expected reward per combination of participation chances. Participant 1 on the bottom row and participant 2 on the top row. It can be observed that higher participation rates yield a higher expected reward, with spikes each time both participation chances reach a relatively high value. This is likely due to the fact that as the product of the probabilities yields the maximum possible chance a state may achieve, reducing the expected reward accordingly. For example, given participants 1 and 2 both have a 0.1 chance to participate, the combination is $0.1 \times 0.1 = 0.01$, meaning the final reward is reduced by x100. Similarly, given participants 1 and 2 both have 0.9 chance to participate, the combination $0.9 \times 0.9 = 0.81$ is significantly higher with at most a 19% reduction. It is also noted that the impact of the tax becomes more pronounced as the probability to purchase increases. This is likely due to participants being taxed more frequently as they are more likely to possess chunks given the higher purchase probability.

Figure 4 shows the probability of reaching the states with the highest and lowest balance. The peaks in the worst (taxed) trend-line may be due to the low purchase likelihood of the participant directly benefiting the other participant, leading the the largest difference in funds. As the purchase probability increases, the peaks reduce in magnitude as probability to reach an equilibrium state increases, decreasing the probability to reach a worst case state. Similarly, the best states are only achievable if neither participant is especially inclined to purchase, increasing the probability of traversing a chain of transitions in which one participant does not purchase chunks, letting the other participant accumulate the rewards unchecked. Figure 5 shows the expected reward as tax increases. As expected, the reward decreases in a linear fashion as the tax increases.

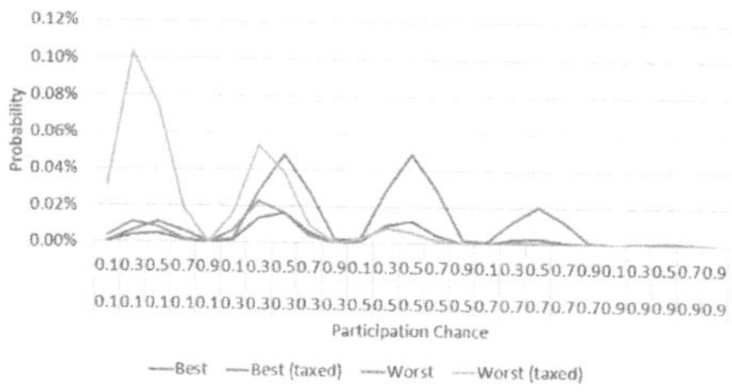

Fig. 4. Probability of reaching state with highest and lowest balance

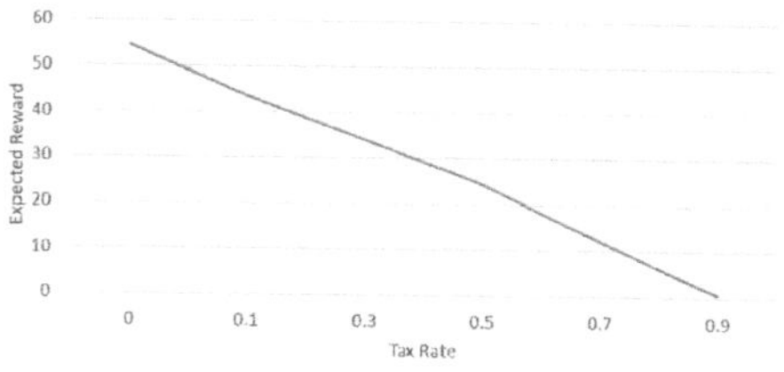

Fig. 5. Expected reward per tax rate

5.2 Simulation

Figures 7 and 6 are the results of a simulation with three participants, four chunks, and limited to 200 rounds. Figure 7 below shows that the general trend is fairly balanced in the beginning but begins to diverge as balances increase. While participant 3 lags behind, this can be explained by the their reduced activity as seen in Fig. 6. Despite this, the average distribution of funds observe a positive trend given the right conditions and do not diverge significantly. As seen in

Fig. 6, the transition of funds occurred fairly frequently, effectively reducing any chance a participant may have in holding all the chunks. It is noted that there were several instances when a participant was able to hold all the chunks. while they were never in a participants possession for longer than a single round, it is less than ideal as it is possible for the game to reach such a state. Despite these spikes, the balances did not experience any sudden jumps in correlation to the possession of all chunks. This is likely due to the trade interval being half that of the block time, meaning a participant will likely have to maintain possession of the chunk for two rounds.

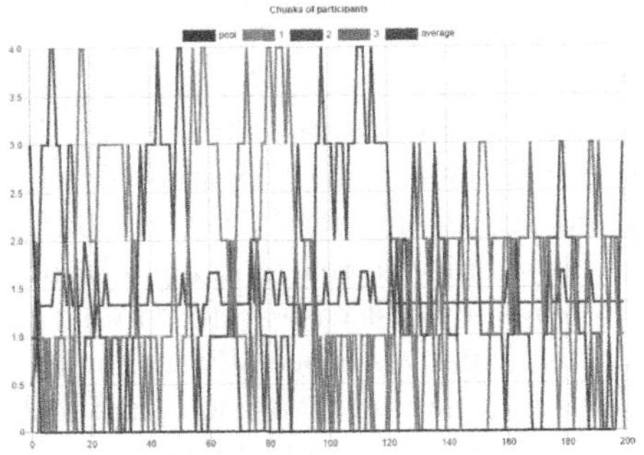

Fig. 6. Chunk distribution over shortened simulation lifespan

Fig. 7. Balance distribution over shortened simulation lifespan

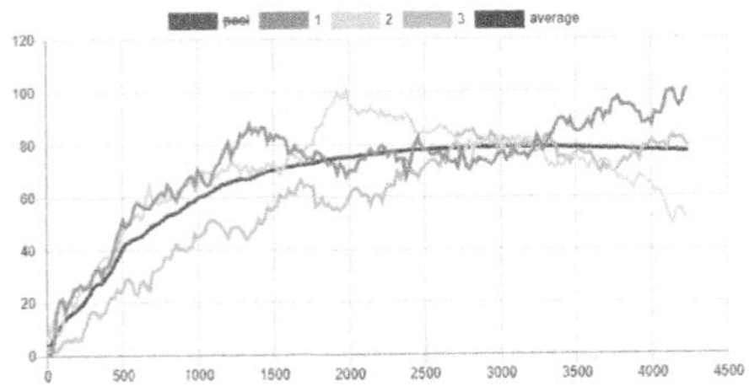

Fig. 8. Balance distribution over simulation lifespan with increased chunks

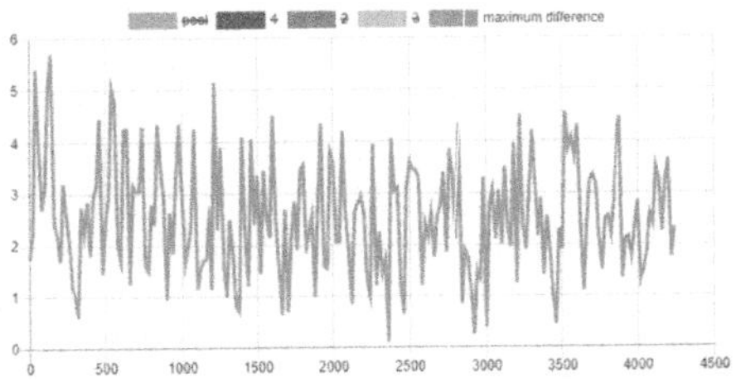

Fig. 9. Averaged chunk distribution over simulation lifespan with increased chunks

Figures 8 and 9 are the results of a simulation with three participants, six chunks, and was allowed to run to completion (based on the discount factor and reward threshold). Figure 8 shows an ideal situation in which despite varying degrees of growth, the final trend is towards the average. It shows that as participants purchase from one another, they may still have chunks in reserve, accumulating rewards passively as they trade as they are able to consistently maintain ownership of chunks for longer. In this case, the balance is likely to converge despite differing participation probabilities as participants effectively inhibit divergence through consistent trading. It is noted that the number of rounds is less than the previous simulation. This is due to the increased number of chunks resulting in lower rewards per chunk as previously defined by Sect. 3.1.

Figure 9 below shows the maximum difference in chunks held over the lifespan of the simulation. Over the course of the simulation, no participant held more all available chunks for longer than one round, reducing the likelihood of earning the whole balance awarded to the pool.

Figures 10 and 11 are the results of a simulation with three participants, two chunks, and was allowed to run to completion (based on the discount factor and reward threshold). As seen in Fig. 10 below, the funds appear to diverge as time goes on with one participant reaching close to an no funds. This is likely due to the fact that as the number of chunks is not enough to satisfy all participants, some participants are not able to receive a reward during some rounds and become disadvantaged due to the difference.

Fig. 10. Balance distribution over simulation lifespan with decreased chunks

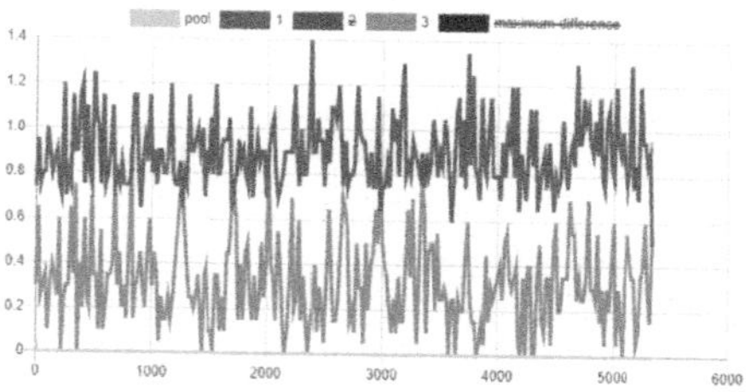

Fig. 11. Comparison of chunk possession by participant 1 and 3 over simulation lifespan with decreased chunks

Figure 11 shows how participant 1 was able to purchase chunks first and immediately gained an advantage with a much higher average chunk count (~0.9). Meanwhile participant 3 was had a much lower average (~0.3), leading to much slower growth. This is the least ideal instance of a game as there is a participant with a disproportionate number of chunks and is able to maintain their advantage fairly effectively.

In general, it can be seen that the ratio of chunks to participants may play a significant role in balancing the ease of achieving equilibrium. Despite the possibilities of significant losses, it is also possible to achieve a fairly distributed game if there exists the opportunity for participants to maintain possession of chunks across rounds.

6 Conclusion and Future Work

The Harberger Tax provides a viable economy as a starting point in ideal conditions. The probability of achieving the equilibrium state and maximising expected reward is heavily dependent on the willingness of a participant to actively engage in trading. However there exist limitations in terms of scalability and longevity as maintaining fairness requires balancing parameters such as taxation, trade interval versus block time, and the number of chunks per participant. The stability and distributed nature is heavily reliant on implementation-specific mechanisms and the effects of integrating with a system that allocates computational power is still unknown. This motivates further improvement in scalability and practical applications.

Appendix

Algorithm 5. Simulation event loop

procedure SIMULATE(G, B, P_ρ, S_ρ)
  $round \leftarrow 0$
  while $R(round) > t$ **do**
    if $round \bmod \left(\left\lfloor \frac{B.b}{P_\rho.t} \right\rfloor\right) \equiv 0$ **then**
      REWARD(S_ρ, B, P_ρ) ▷ refer to algorithm 6
    end if
    $bidders \leftarrow \{b \in S_\rho \mid b.balance \geq 1\}$
    for $p \in \{p \in S_\rho \mid p.chunks \geq 1\}$ **do**
      AUCTION($bidders, p$) ▷ refer to algorithm 7
    end for
    $round \leftarrow round + 1$
  end while
end procedure

Algorithm 6. Reward system for pool participants

procedure REWARD(S_ρ, B, P_ρ)
  $roll \leftarrow$ RANDOMFLOAT(0, 1) ▷ a random decimal in the range [0, 1]
  if $roll > \frac{P_\rho.H}{B.\mathbb{H}}$ **then**
    return ▷ Pool did not validate the block
  end if
  $leftover \leftarrow r$
  for $\rho \in S_\rho$ **do**
    $amount \leftarrow R(\rho.chunks)$ ▷ refer to section 3.1
    $\rho.funds \leftarrow \rho.funds + amount$
    $leftover \leftarrow leftover - amount$
  end for
  $P_\rho.funds \leftarrow P_\rho.funds + leftover$
end procedure

Algorithm 7. Recursive auction resolution

```
procedure AUCTION(B, ρ_s, price, ρ_b)
    if B = ∅ then
        ρ_b.funds ← ρ_b.funds − price
        ρ_b.ownedChunks ← ρ_b.ownedChunks + 1
        ρ_s.funds ← ρ_s.funds + price
        ρ_s.ownedChunks ← ρ_s.ownedChunks − 1
        return
    end if
    bidder_max ← ρ_b
    bid_max ← price
    for bidder ∈ B do
        bid ← bidder.BID(price)
        if bid > bid_max then
            bid_max ← bid
            bidder_max ← bidder
        end if
    end for
    B′ ← ∅
    for bidder ∈ B do
        p ← CHECKPARTICIPATION(bidder, ρ_s, bid_max, bidder_max)    ▷ refer to algorithm 8
        if p = true then
            B′ ← B′ ∪ bidder
        end if
    end for
    return AUCTION(B′, ρ_s, bid_max, bidder_max)
end procedure
```

Algorithm 8. Participant decision making process

```
procedure CHECKPARTICIPATION(B, ρ_s, price, ρ_b, round)
    if ρ = ρ_s ∨ ρ = ρ_b ∨ price > ρ.funds
        ∨ (WANTEDCHUNKS ∈ ρ.σ
        ∧ ρ.ownedChunks ≥ ρ.wantedChunks)
        ∨ (SKIPFIRST ∈ ρ.σ
        ∧ round = 0)  then
        return false
    end if
    if FIRST ∈ ρ.σ ∧ round = 0 then
        return true
    end if
    if ALTERNATE ∈ ρ.σ then
        if (FIRST ∈ ρ.σ ∧ round (mod 2) = 0)
            ∨ (SKIPFIRST ∈ ρ.σ ∧ round (mod 2) ≠ 0)  then
            return true
        end if
    end if
    if CHANCE ∈ ρ.σ ∧ RANDOMFLOAT(0, 1) < ρ.chance then
        return true
    end if
    return false
end procedure
```

References

1. Hashrate distribution. https://www.blockchain.com/pools
2. Market capitalization. https://www.blockchain.com/charts/market-cap
3. Total hash rate (th/s). https://www.blockchain.com/charts/hash-rate
4. Ghash.io (2019). http://web.archive.org/web/20200111195539/http://ghash.io/
5. Cambridge bitcoin electricity consumption index (2020). https://www.cbeci.org/
6. Back, A.: Hashcash - A denial of service counter-measure. Technical report

7. Bastiaan, M.: Preventing the 51%-attack: a stochastic analysis of two phase proof of work in bitcoin (2015)
8. Beikverdi, A., Song, J.: Trend of centralization in bitcoin's distributed network. In: 2015 IEEE/ACIS 16th International Conference on Software Engineering, Artificial Intelligence, Networking and Parallel/Distributed Computing (SNPD), pp. 1–6 (2015)
9. Leonardos, N., Leonardos, S., Piliouras, G.: Oceanic games: centralization risks and incentives in blockchain mining. In: Mathematical Research for Blockchain Economy, pp. 183–199 (2020)
10. Luu, L., Velner, Y., Teutsch, J., Saxena, P.: Smartpool: practical decentralized pooled mining. In: Proceedings of the 26th USENIX Conference on Security Symposium, pp. 1409–1426 (2017)
11. Microsoft: TypeScript. https://www.typescriptlang.org/
12. Nakamoto, S.: Bitcoin: a peer-to-peer electronic cash system. Technical report (2009)
13. Osborne, M.J., Rubinstein, A.: A Course in Game Theory. The MIT Press (1994)
14. Posner, E.A., Weyl, E.G.: Property is only another name for monopoly. J. Legal Anal. **9**(1), 51–123 (2017)
15. Source, O.: Mermaid. https://mermaid-js.github.io/
16. Source, O.: P2pool. http://p2pool.in/

Blockchain Based Electrical Vehicle Charging Platform

Chensheng Zhu, Naipeng Dong(✉), and Guangdong Bai

The University of Queensland, St Lucia, Brisbane, QLD, Australia
chensheng.zhu@uq.net.au, {n.dong,g.bai}@uq.edu.au

Abstract. The revolution of electrical vehicles is accelerating, occupying increasingly larger market. The government's policy announcement to encourage the development of electric vehicles has also accelerated the development of electric vehicles. As a result, the demand for charging stations in cities with large populations is increasing. Studies have shown that customers worry that the lack of charging stations is the third biggest obstacle to buying electric vehicles. One solution is to use personal chargers. Although most private electric car chargers are used for slow charging of light vehicles, these chargers can still provide considerable charging speed (up to 44 mph), and most of them are idle. Existing traditional charging sharing transaction platforms have potential security and privacy issues. In order to solve these problems and integrate private charging stations, this work aims to design and build a trusted and transparent blockchain and smart contract based charging sharing transaction platform.

Keywords: Blockchain · Electrical Vehicle Charging · DApp

1 Introduction

The revolution of electric vehicle (EV) is speeding up, global sales of electric vehicles is 2.1 million in 2019 [3] and 14 million in 2023 [2]. In 2019 electric vehicles accounted for 2.6% of global vehicle sales [1] and became around 18% of all cars sold in 2023 [2]. Government policy announcements also accelerate the development of electric vehicles, for instance, direct subsidies, and policy enforcement such as zero-mission vehicles mandates and fuel economy standards [1].

Compared to conventional petrol or diesel car, electric vehicle has a lower maintenance cost. The most concern regarding battery worn out and replacement has been addressed by that most electric vehicle manufacturers warrant EV batteries for around 8 years [6]. Another concern however remains that in cities with large populations, the demand for charge stations is grating. For example, Los Angeles requires 35000 additional charge points in 2017 [5]. The concern that the lack of charge stations is the third most serious barrier to EV purchase.

Although the number of electrical vehicles charging stations grows fast, with about 7.3 million chargers worldwide. However, among them, 6.5 million are

S. Kanhere et al. (Eds.): SDLT 2024, CCIS 2453, pp. 103–116, 2025.
https://doi.org/10.1007/978-981-96-4442-1_7

private [1]. Therefore, ChargeHub is developed, which is a mobile app that allows sharing electric vehicle charge stations [8]. Although most of the electric vehicle chargers are used for light-duty vehicles slow charging, the slow chargers still can provide up to 44 miles/hour charging speed [4], and most of them are under idle time. Once setting up the app, the private charge station will display on the map in the app, and users can contact to charge station owner to coordinate charging.

However, this traditional charging sharing market may result in some potential security and privacy issues [7]:

1. The lack of transparency of essential information and data to the users, including, the responsibility of contractors, documents and reports, charge fees etc.
2. Centralized Structure - The centralized structure of the existing services incurs costs to both the owners and users at the same time. The middlemen may drive out small businesses and generate a false monopoly in the market for example, by charging high commissions.
3. The lack of trust - There is a significant absence of trust in the centralised charging business. Proprietors frequently expect users to pay robust sums in time, but they neglect to keep their pledge when these deposits are made. On the other hand, the users occupied the parking area over time in some circumstances, but disagree to pay the appropriate bills.

To solve these problems and integrate the private charging stations, this work aims to design and build a trusted and transparent decentralized sharing transaction system, based on blockchain [9,11,12] and smart contract, for the following reasons.

First, the decentralized system is different from the traditional central payment system, it lowers the cost of trade by eliminating third parties to mediate among the prosumers [13], and every transaction will be publicly cryptographically recorded, this helps build the peer-to-peer (P2P) transactions between EV owners and charge stations [13].

Second, due to most private charge stations are installed at home, the owners' safety needs to be protected by ensuring confidence of consumers' repudiation. The distributed peer-to-peer blockchain transaction system can help solve this problem. Compared with the traditional sharing trading platform, peer-to-peer decentralized system doesn't build based on any sever, all the data will be saved on blockchain, and the recording on blockchain is cryptographically secure and immutable [10]. This guarantees that the bad behaviours of any consumer will be recorded and cannot be changed, which facilitates a trusted and healthy ecosystem.

Third, due to there isn't an intermediary, the system is unsupervised. In order to design an open self-executing and fair of trading platform, this system is built based on smart contract. Smart contract is the computer code that can execute automatically, and it is publicly recorded on the blockchain [14]. When certain criteria are satisfied, the smart contract will execute the step triggered, and the details will be recorded on blockchain [14]. This guarantees the transaction system to be secure and self-executing.

2 Related Work

This section will focus on several different blockchain-based electrical vehicle charging trading platform or power grid energy trading platform.

In the current traditional centralized transaction system, user's personal information and data is saved unilaterally in central servers [16]. And compared with that, in decentralized and distributed blockchain-base transaction system, the data is saved on blockchain [15]. The blocks that saved data is secured and bound to each other through the utilization of the cryptographic principles, and the database is managed by a large number of nodes that doesn't owned by any single entity [15]. Therefore, some researchers hope to apply the blockchain-based transaction platform to electric vehicle charging transaction systems to deal with energy transaction management and handle some essential issues such as the lack of trust.

The work [18] designed an electric vehicle (EV) and charge station (CS) integrated system that consists of 4 parts, a vehicle infotainment system (ITS), a sealed-bid auction system, a EV-BC smart contract and a EVCS-BC smart contract. When user sends a charging request to the system, the ITS will provide a list of potential CS based on the default route and its location. And their Ethereum addresses will be sent to the EV-BC contract, and bids request will be sent to CS smart contract correspondingly. Through such a workflow, a "negative" blind auction has been organized. This research simply designed a simple electric vehicle charging autonomous selection system and develop the smart contract, but is not implemented as a entire system/application. It only considers simple use-cases of blockchain based EV charging system, and the design of smart contract only concerned the cost. More factors should be considered to improve the entire process, as pointed in [17].

The work [17] also introduced a blockchain-based electrical vehicle charging trading platform. But compared with [16], the authors provide a more complex design of smart contract. To avoid issues like the lack of trust, a punishment and compensation system is designed. Owing to the viable information from EVs, the system is able to create a dynamic mechanism system to do the cost calculation for the charging of each EV. Interference and trust lack issues have also been optimized along with the execution of the smart contract. In the system, each EV finds a suitable charge station, and the emerging transaction is also in processing. However, if the EV arrive charge station late, then the smart contract will reevaluate his charging cost. In this situation, a penalty factor will be added to his total cost as punishment. And if the CS is not able to provide charging service, the smart contract will also reevaluate EV's charging cost to reimburse customers.

The proposed charging trading blockchain-based system in [19] is similar to the one proposed in [17]. But they have some specific contribution and differences.

- To ensure that every node has a copy of the recognized version of the whole ledger. The work [19] apply the DBFT algorithm to the blockchain-based trading platform to reach the consensus efficiently.

- The work [19] designed a smart contract to coordinates EV charging system operating way to achieve a higher operator utility [10].

According to [20], the researchers proposed a new EV charging mode, where EV doesn't need to charge instead of switching a depleted battery to a fully charged one, it can save the EV charging time. Based on that, the researchers designed a EV charging blockchain trading system. But here comes some problems about (1) lacking trust between EV drivers and the charge stations; (2) fairness and justice in the battery swapping process procedure [20]. The authors considered that blockchain-based trading platform becomes the optimal solution. They designed a smart contract for

- Battery process: A mechanism is created and built to calculate the factor of the battery's deprecation rate (to guarantee the fairness of transaction).
- Balance Process: When the user send a transaction to swap EV battery, the smart contract will calculate the price differences based on the battery quality estimation.
- Battery Interface: It is used for read the data of Battery and provide some fundamental system functions.

The detailed analysis of the deployment of the system environment along with the related experiments inspired our work. But their energy refuelling mode is different from ours.

3 Background

Blockchain is an open decentralized ledger, and the ledger is managed by a large number of nodes that doesn't owned by any single entity [15]. Each of these data blocks of data is secured and linked with previous block by cryptographic principles [15]. The ledger is reproducible and shared, all the information on blocks is public cryptographically recorded [22]. The data structure of blockchain is a chain list of blocks with transaction details [21].

3.1 Consensus

The consensus algorithm is very important in the blockchain, and its existence allows users to coordinate in a distributed setting. It can ensure that all agents in the system can agree on the transaction history, even if some agents fail [23]. In the blockchain network, transaction information will be publicly recorded on the blockchain. Every node must maintain the same copy of the blockchain, which is crucial [23]. Otherwise, the conflicting information records will end-up the same copy, and the blockchain network will also be destroyed [23].

In blockchain network, the user who added the block (the validator) is asked to provide a stake. The stake is the value that a validator must offer to ensure them will act honestly. If they cheat, they will lose their stake [23]. And the validators can get rewards. It usually consists of the native cryptocurrency of the protocol, and is composed of fees paid by other users, new generated cryptocurrency units, or both [23]. To ensure the transparency of blockchain. Some nodes should be able to supervise the validators. Adding blocks on blockchain will cost a lot, but it's free for anyone to read data form blockchain and verify them [23]. This ensures that the validators is checked by any other users.

3.2 Ethereum

With the development of blockchain, bitcoin is no longer the only application of blockchain [24]. Based on blockchain, people developed some decentralized applications other than digital currencies. Ethereum is a popular open blockchain platform, that helps developers communicate between blockchain and smart contract. And it provided programming language Solidity to write smart contract. It is very useful for decentralized application development.

3.3 Web3.js

Web3.js is the library that provides several API for developers to communicate with Ethereum Vehicle Node [25]. To develop a decentralized application based on Ethereum, web3.js is an essential part. Developers can get cache status, account information, call the Ethereum tokens, or monitor events by web3.js [25]. Several common functions on web3.js that are used in this work are listed:

- web3.eth.getCoinbase(): get users Ethereum account address;
- web3.eth.getBalance(): get users ETH balance;
- web3.sendTransaction(): can transfer ETH from users account to another account
- web3.version.getNode(): get the status of users Ethereum node.
- web3.personal.lockAccount()/web3.personal.unlockAccount(): lock or unlock a specific Ethereum account.
- web3.eth.contract(abi): deploy a smart contract, the abi is the API of smart contract.

3.4 Smart Contract

Smart contracts were first introduced by Nick Szabo, a computer scientist and cryptographer [14]. He defined that smart contract is the computerized transaction protocols contract. And now, the smart contract is the computer code that can execute automatically, and it is publicly recorded on the blockchain platform. And the code reproducible and shared on all nodes of a blockchain platform [14]. Hence, the patterns of security, permanence and immutability which are offered by the blockchain are beneficial for smart contract [14].

Smart contracts are also a type of Ethereum account [26]. This means that they have Ethereum account balance and can also send transactions to other accounts. However, they cannot be controlled by other users, they are deployed on Ethereum network and run according to code. Users on other nodes can interact with the smart contract by sending a transaction that performs the functions defined on the smart contract [26].

4 System Design

This project aims to integrate private charge stations to design and build a sharing charging transaction system. The system is based on the existing blockchain platform—Ethereum, which is the most popular open-source blockchain platform, and support smart contract functionality. This decentralized system helps solve the following potential problems:

- Transparency: The transaction details are publicly recorded on smart contract, including appointment time, charging cost, leaving time, charge station id...
- Trust issue: Before sending a transaction request, users must send a 0.5 ETH deposit to smart contract account. After the payment finish successfully, the deposit will be returned to the users' Ethereum account, otherwise, the user can't get his deposit back. Also if the user occupies the charge station over time, he should pay extra for punishment.

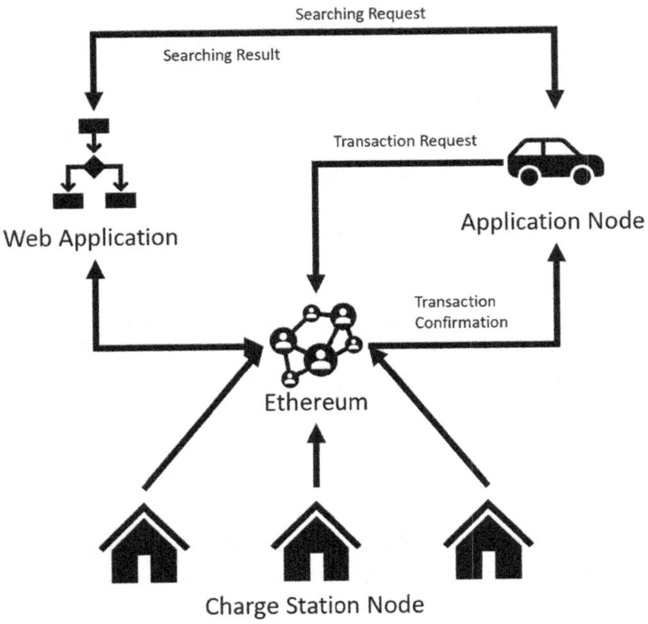

Fig. 1. System Architecture.

4.1 System Architecture

The system mainly contains four parts, Application Node, Charge Station Node, Smart Contract, and web app. And the System Architecture Diagram (Fig. 1) describes how users and charge stations interact on this EV-CS P2P transaction system.

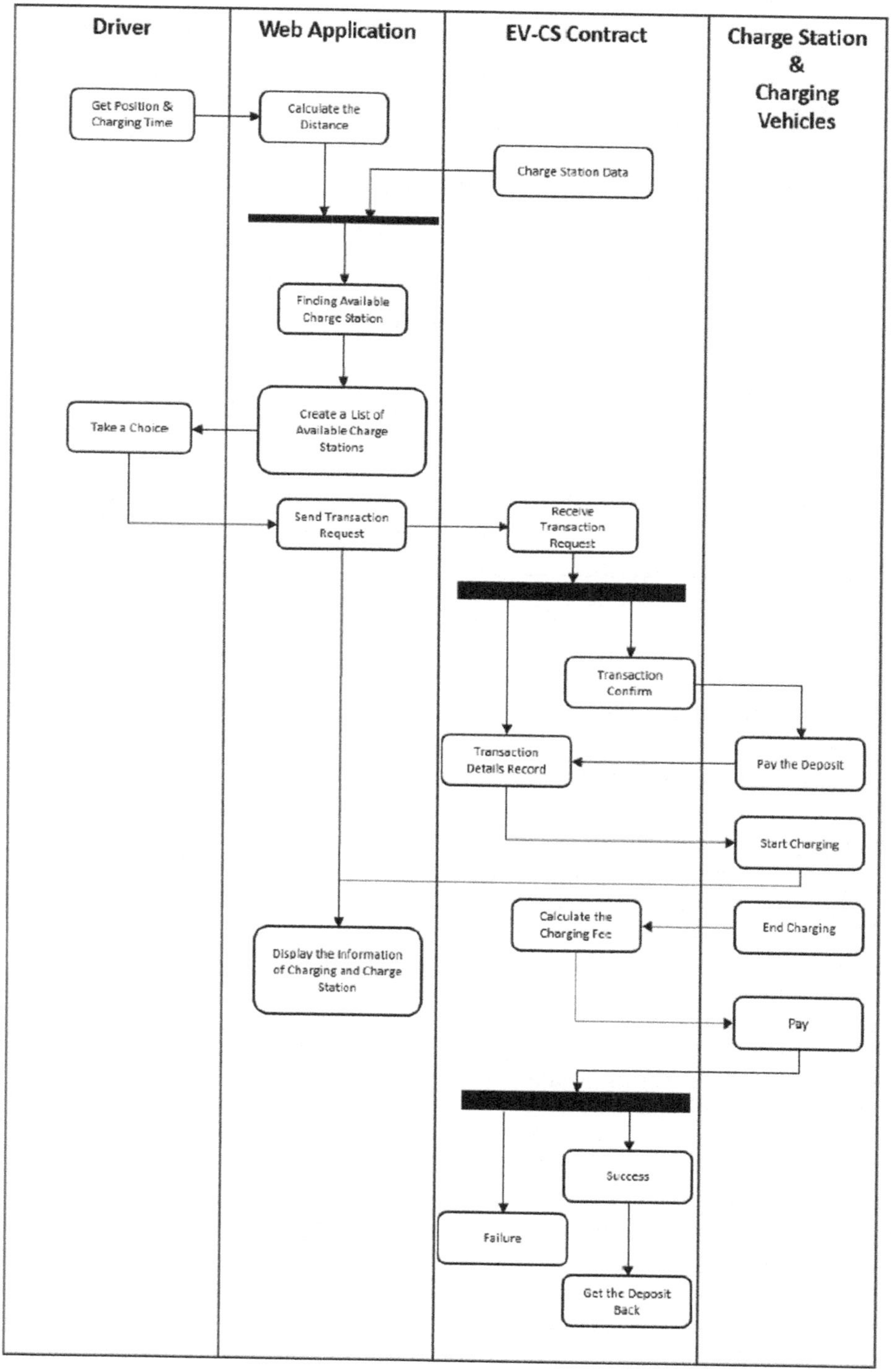

Fig. 2. Application Node Work Flow.

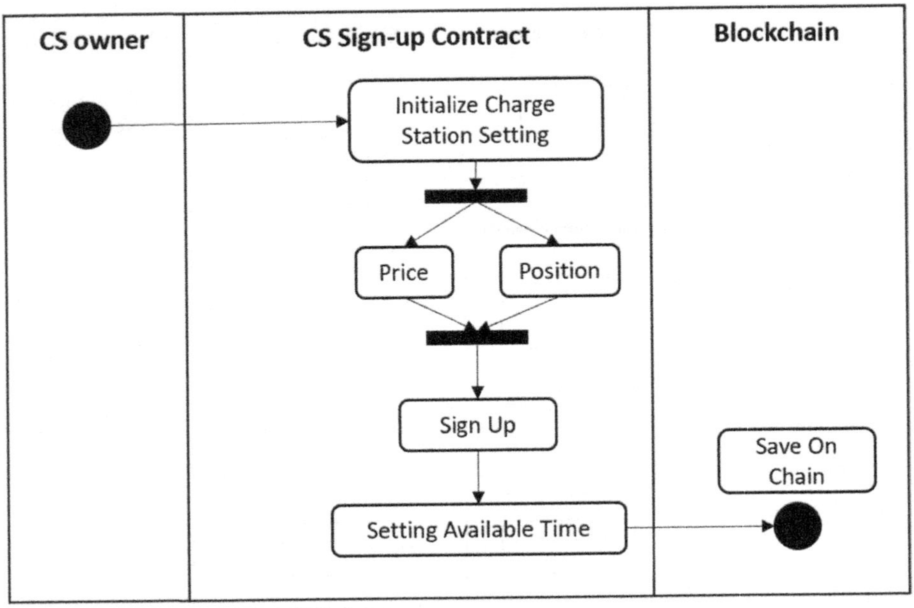

Fig. 3. Charge Station Node Work flow.

Charge Station Node: The Charge Station Node is used for charge stations to sign-up and initialized. The Ethereum address, charging price, location and available time zone should be public recorded on blockchain, and these data can be read by Application Node. This guarantee the fairness and openness of this p2p transaction system, all the data recorded on blockchain are immutable and cryptographically secure. And the workflow diagram is shown in Fig. 3.

Because the charge station node is only used to record the data on blockchain, and there isn't a web application designed for charge station node. The charge station set-up procedure is involved in the constructor of the smart contract.

Application Node: The Application Node is designed for electrical vehicle drivers to use by the web application. The web application will read user's requirements and get the charge station data from blockchain. Then, according to users' requests to find out the available charge stations and create a list. The users can select a preferred charge station and send a transaction request to blockchain. And, due to the transaction transparency, the transaction details will be publicly recorded on blockchain. To ensure the fairness of transaction, before sending the transaction request are confirmed, users should pay the deposit, the deposit is saved on the smart contract. Now, the transaction start. The information on transaction and charging station will be displayed on the web application. When charging is finished, the users should pay the charging fee, the charging fee is based on users' charging time. If users stop charging before the appointment end time, and only need to pay for booking time. If charging is overtime, users are required to pay some extra. After the payment is finished successfully, the deposit will be returned to the user's account. The workflow of Application node is shown in Fig. 2.

5 Implementation and Discussion

5.1 System Implementation

A prototype system is implemented for the decentralized private charge station sharing transaction system based on Ethereum, using Ganache to simulate the blockchain network [27–29]. It contains the following three main parts:

1. Users HTML Pages
   - index.html: welcome login page for users;
   - login.html: searching available charge station send charging request;
   - time.html: display charging information and pay charge fee; transactionFinish.html: display transaction information after charging success.
2. Interact (app.js)
3. Smart Contract (election.sol) And this implementation aims to demonstrate:
   - Users are able to send a transaction to smart contract.
   - Charge stations are able to set up on smart contract.
   - The data are able to publicly record on blockchain and gas fee free to read by users.
   - Users are able to pay for charging.
   - The deposit can be saved on smart contract.
   - The deposit can be returned automatically from smart contract to users' account.

   The following diagram in Fig. 4 shows the interaction between the functions in web app and smart contract:

5.2 Gas Cost Discussion

In blockchain and smart contract, users are required to pay the gas fee to compensate for the computing energy required to process and validate transactions on the Ethereum [30]. To achieve information security and transaction system fairness, all data should be recorded on blockchain and all the functions should be written on smart contract. Too much data recording and computing will generate a high gas fee [30]. The transaction system in this work faces this problem in the function *findChargeStation* and tries to figure out how to take the balance between operation cost and trade security and fairness.

The function *findChargeStation* is designed to filter out suitable charge stations for users based on their requirements. Originally, this function is implemented in smart contracts. This design has 5 mainly drawbacks:

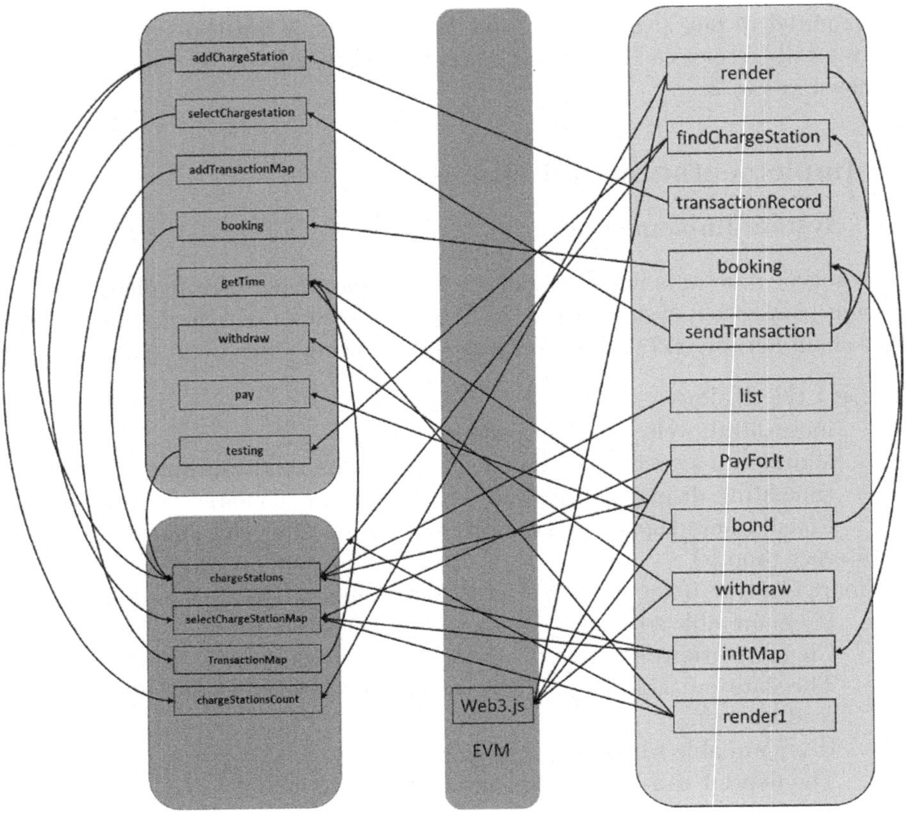

Fig. 4. Function Interaction.

1. The calculation of the distance between charge stations and users will generate a big gas fee cost. There are only three value types contained in Solidity, bool, integer and address, float or double is not acceptable. But my system use latitude and longitude to record the location of the charge station, and they are the decimal retain 8 digits. And to save the latitude and longitude on smart contract. I multiply them by 100000000. The results are that the distance computation becomes more complex calculation and takes more computing energy.
2. The more charge station saved on blockchain; the more distance calculation and data record will be generated.
3. The computation energy cost is related to booking hours.
4. Save the searching results on blockchain will generate gas fee.
5. Some users may send many times searching requests before making a choice and the function findChargeStation will also be called many times. It will waste a huge amount of gas fee.

To avoid generating too much gas fee for computing and data recording, I optimized my smart contract and web application–migrate the function findChargeStation from smart contract to web application.

Reading the data from blockchain will not charge any gas fee. Reading the data of the charge station (id, location, price, available time) and filter out the available charge station on JavaScript will charge no gas fee. This design decision achieves the same functionality. The difference is when checking whether the charge station satisfies user's time requisition, more variables are used.

5.3 Experiment and Results

Two experiments are conducted to show the performance of the system regarding gas fee.

First, the prototype system is tested on the gas fee against the number of charging stations. The result is shown in Fig. 5. The result clearly shows that with the increase of charge station number, the gas fee generated is increased linearly.

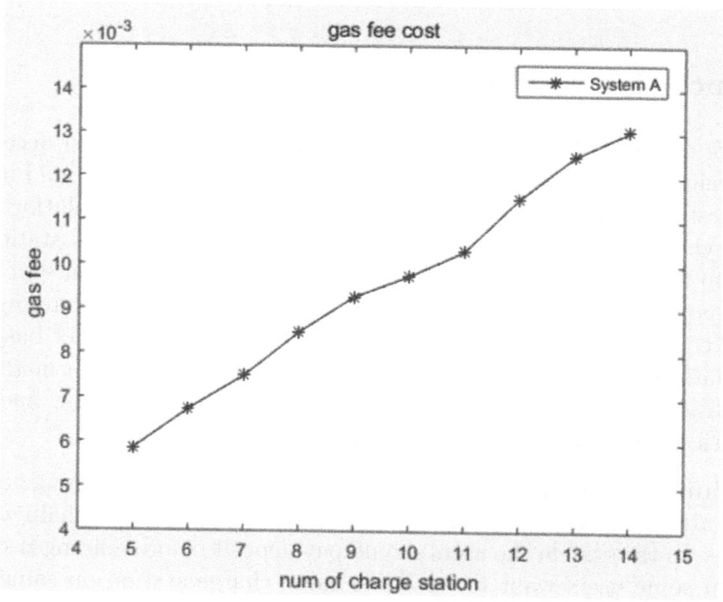

Fig. 5. Evaluation of gas fee against the number of charging stations.

Second, we compared the previous two designs: implementing *findChargeStation* on smart contract (System A) and implementing findChargeStation on web App (system B) with 6 charge stations on blockchain. Table 1 shows the generated gas fee cost for System A and system B.

Table 1. Gas fee comparision of two different designs.

Function	System A gas fee	System B gas fee
findChargeStation()	0.006745	NA
selectChargeStation()	0.000811	0.000811
transactionRecors()	0.001061	0.000811
booking()	0.001165	0.001165
bond()	0.0006	0.0006
payForIt()	0.00042	0.00042
withdraw()	0.000946	0.000946
Sum:	0.011747	0.005002

Compared the result with the experiment, it's obvious that findChargeStation() cost expensive gas fee, it because that this function calculate the distance between users location to every charge station and check state of the charge station every hour from appointment start time to end time. And float type is not acceptable in smart contract, it takes higher gas fee for distance computation.

6 Conclusion and Future Work

This work designs a trusted blockchain and smart contract based decentralized electric vehicle charge station sharing transaction platform, and build it on local private testing Ethereum network. This decentralized trading platform is consisted of charge station node and application node. The charge station owner can set-up their charge stations on blockchain, and the users can find out suitable charge station based on their requirement, and then send charging request to smart contract. As a result, this blockchain and smart contract based transaction platform solved the potential security and privacy issues in traditional sharing trading platform. It integrate the private charge station, and provide the electric vehicle drivers better charging experience.

Limitations and Future Work. The evaluation ignores the Mining node in the local private Ethereum network, they are the key point for blockchain wallet and currencies. In the system the users should pay deposit before sending transaction. But when some users want to book the same charge station on same time. It will result a system conflict. The next step is to solve these problems. It would be also interesting to see how to guarantee that the state of charge station send to blockchain is reliable and security.

References

1. IEA: "Global EV Outlook 2020 – Analysis," IEA. https://www.iea.org/reports/global-ev-outlook-2020. Accessed 07 Nov 2020

2. Trends in electric cars. https://www.iea.org/reports/global-ev-outlook-2024/trends-in-electric-cars. Accessed 03 Nov 11 2024
3. Markets, R.: "Global Electric Cars Market Report (2020 to 2030) - COVID-19 Growth and Change," GlobeNewswire News Room, 29-Jun-2020. https://www.globenewswire.com/news-release/2020/06/29/2054682/0/en/Global-Electric-Cars-Market-Report-2020-to-2030-COVID-19-Growth-and-Change.html. Accessed 07 Nov 2020
4. Wall Connector. https://shop.tesla.com/product/wall-connector. Accessed 07 Nov 2020
5. Marshall, A.: "The US Cites That Need More Electric-Car Charging Stations, Mapped," Wired, 25-Jan-2019. https://www.wired.com/story/us-charging-network-electric-vehicle-needs/. Accessed 07 Nov 2020
6. "Benefits Of Electric Cars," Ergon Energy. https://www.ergon.com.au/network/smarter-energy/electric-vehicles/benefits-of-electric-vehicles. Accessed 07 Nov 2020
7. Hassija, V., Zaid, M., Singh, G., Srivastava, A., Saxena, V.: Cryptober: a blockchain-based secure and cost-optimal car rental platform. In: 2019 Twelfth International Conference on Contemporary Computing (IC3), Noida, India, 2019, pp. 1–6 (2019). https://doi.org/10.1109/IC3.2019.8844943.
8. ChargeHub: "The Top 8 most popular charging stations," ChargeHub. https://chargehub.com/en/. Accessed 07 Nov 2020
9. Tummalacherla, P.: Blockchain: the game-Changing Technology in Web 3.0, Medium, 09-Aug-2019. https://medium.com/@IamPremt/blockchain-the-game-changing-technology-in-web-3-0-6761d1531b57. Accessed 07 Nov 2020
10. MLSDev: Blockchain architecture basics: components, structure, benefits & creation. Medium, 07-Mar-2019. https://mlsdev.medium.com/blockchain-architecture-basics-components-structure-benefits-creation-beace17c8e77. Accessed 07 Nov 2020
11. Reiff, N.: Blockchain explained, Investopedia, 31-Aug-2020. https://www.investopedia.cFig 0-1om/terms/b/blockchain.asp. Accessed 07 Nov 2020
12. Narayanan, A., Bonneau, J., Felten, E., Miller, A., Goldfeder, S.: Bitcoin and Cryptocurrency Technologies: A Comprehensive Introduction. Princeton University Press (2016)
13. Thakur, S., Breslin, J.G.: Cost Analysis of blockchains-based peer to peer energy trade. In: 2020 IEEE International Conference on Environment and Electrical Engineering and 2020 IEEE Industrial and Commercial Power Systems Europe (EEEIC / I&CPS Europe), Madrid, Spain, pp. 1–6 (2020)
14. Lipton, A., Levi, S.: An introduction to smart contracts and their potential and inherent limitations. The Harvard Law School Forum on Corporate Governance, 26-May-2018. https://corpgov.law.harvard.edu/2018/05/26/an-introduction-to-smart-contracts-and-their-potential-and-inherent-limitations/. Accessed 07 Nov 2020
15. Rosic, A.: "What is Blockchain Technology? A Step-by-Step Guide For Beginners," Blockgeeks, 29-Oct-2020. https://blockgeeks.com/guides/what-is-blockchain-technology/. Accessed 07 Nov 2020
16. "File server: definition and basics," IONOS Digitalguide. https://www.ionos.com/digitalguide/server/know-how/file-server/. Accessed 07 Nov 2020
17. Asfia, U., Kamuni, V., Sheikh, A., Wagh, S., Patel, D.: Energy trading of electric vehicles using blockchain and smart contracts. In: 2019 18th European Control Conference (ECC), 25-28 June 2019, pp. 3958–3963 (2019)

18. Pustišek, M., Kos, A., Sedlar, U.: Blockchain based autonomous selection of electric vehicle charging station. In: 2016 International Conference on Identification, Information and Knowledge in the Internet of Things (IIKI), 20-21 Oct 2016, pp. 217–222 (2016)
19. Wang, Y., Su, Z., Xu, Q., Zhang, N.: Contract based energy blockchain for secure electric vehicles charging in smart community. In: 2018 IEEE 16th International Conference on Dependable, Autonomic and Secure Computing, 16th International Conference on Pervasive Intelligence and Computing, 4th International Conference on Big Data Intelligence and Computing and Cyber Science and Technology Congress(DASC/PiCom/DataCom/CyberSciTech), 12-15 Aug. 2018, pp. 323–327 (2018)
20. Hua, S., Zhou, E., Pi, B., Sun, J., Nomura, Y., Kurihara, H.: Apply blockchain technology to electric vehicle battery refueling. In: HICSS (2018)
21. Blockchain architecture explained: how it works & how to build. https://mlsdev.com/blog/156-how-to-build-your-own-blockchain-architecture. Accessed 07 Nov 2020
22. "Asymmetric Cryptography In Blockchains," Hacker Noon, 05-Nov-2020. https://hackernoon.com/asymmetric-cryptography-in-blockchains-d1a4c1654a71. Accessed 07 Nov 2020
23. Binance Academy: "What Is a Blockchain Consensus Algorithm?," Binance Academy, 01-Jul-2020. https://academy.binance.com/en/articles/what-is-a-blockchain-consensus-algorithm. Accessed 07 Nov 2020
24. "What Are The Blockchain's Limitations?," FXCM Markets, 20-Aug-2019. https://www.fxcm.com/markets/insights/what-are-blockchains-limitations/. Accessed 07 Nov 2020
25. "web3.eth," web3.eth - web3.js 1.0.0 documentation. https://web3js.readthedocs.io/en/v1.2.0/web3-eth.html. Accessed 07 Nov 2020
26. "Introduction to smart contracts," ethereum.org. https://ethereum.org/en/developers/docs/smart-contracts/. Accessed 07 Nov 2020
27. Truffle Suite, "Ganache: Overview: Documentation," Truffle Suite. https://www.trufflesuite.com/docs/ganache/overview. Accessed 07 Nov 2020
28. Škvorc, B.: "Developing for ethereum: getting started with ganache," Codementor. https://www.codementor.io/@swader/developing-for-ethereum-getting-started-with-ganache-l6abwh62j. Accessed 07 Nov 2020
29. Go Ethereum. https://geth.ethereum.org/. Accessed 07 Nov 2020
30. Frankenfield, J.: (2020, September 30). Gas (Ethereum) https://www.investopedia.com/terms/g/gas-ethereum.asp. Accessed 16 Oct 2020

Industry Track

Water Ledger: A Blockchain-Based Smart Water Resource Management Platform

Katrina Donaghy(✉), Zhaojin Li, and Farhad-Ullah Rezwan

Water Ledger Australia, Level 18 Waterfront Place, 1 Eagle Street, Brisbane Q 4000, Australia
katrina@civicledger.com

Abstract. The Third-Generation Blockchain Technique has been widely adopted in large amounts of applications, due to its better performance compared to traditional Proof-of-Work mechanisms. However, few practitioners focus on water, which is one of the most important resources for people and has been largely wasted due to lack of properties like transparency, trust, and bad management. Hence, in this paper, we introduce our new application: Water Ledger, which is built based on web3 techniques and aims to solve the problems above. Water Ledger utilizes blockchain technology, specifically the innovative ERC3525 semi-fungible token standard, to create a transparent, efficient, and user-centric platform for water resource accounting, management and trading. This paper presents the architecture of Water Ledger, its implementation of ERC3525 tokens for water rights accounting and management. Our findings suggest that Water Ledger has the potential to revolutionize water resource management by enhancing transparency, improving efficiency, and empowering individual water users.

Keywords: Water · Blockchain Technology · Semi Fungible Token · Water Right · Governance. Accountability · Transparency · Trust

1 Introduction

Water scarcity is an escalating global crisis, with far-reaching implications for food security, public health, and economic stability. The United Nations projects that by 2050 [1], more than 5 billion people could be living in areas suffering from water scarcity, emphasizing the urgent need for innovative solutions in water resource management.

Traditional water management systems face numerous challenges:

1. **Fragmentation**: Water resources are often managed by multiple agencies with overlapping jurisdictions, leading to inefficiencies and conflicts.
2. **Opacity**: Lack of transparency in water allocation and usage data hinders effective decision-making and public trust.
3. **Inefficiency**: Manual processes and outdated technologies result in slow, costly, and error-prone water management.
4. **Inequity**: Current systems often fail to ensure fair access to water resources, particularly for smaller users or disadvantaged communities.

S. Kanhere et al. (Eds.): SDLT 2024, CCIS 2453, pp. 119–124, 2025.
https://doi.org/10.1007/978-981-96-4442-1_8

Blockchain technology, with its inherent properties of transparency, immutability, and decentralization, offers a promising solution to these challenges. While blockchain has been applied in various sectors, its potential in water resource management remains largely unexplored.

This paper introduces Water Ledger [2], an innovative blockchain-based platform developed by Water Ledger Global to revolutionize water resource management. Water Ledger leverages advanced blockchain technology, including the novel ERC3525 semi-fungible token standard, to create a transparent, efficient, and user-centric system for managing water rights and allocations.

The remainder of this paper is structured as follows: Sect. 2 provides an overview of the Water Ledger platform. Section 3 delves into the blockchain technology underpinning Water Ledger, with a focus on the implementation of ERC3525 tokens. Finally, Sect. 4 concludes the paper and outlines future research directions.

2 Introduction

Water Ledger is designed to transform water resource accounting, management, and trading by creating a decentralized, transparent, and efficient marketplace for water rights governance. The platform's core philosophy is to empower individual water users while maintaining regulatory oversight and ensuring sustainable water use.

2.1 Key Features

Water Ledger incorporates several innovative features:

1. **Individual Water Wallets**: Digital wallets allow users to assert and evidence their water rights, declare management actions, and record water usage. These wallets serve as a comprehensive record of a user's water-related activities and entitlements.
2. **Water Resource System (WRS) Administration Wallets**: Administrative functions enable water operators and authorities to define water resource systems, set sustainable yield limits, and manage restrictions on water use. This ensures that the platform aligns with regulatory requirements and environmental considerations.
3. **Community Water Exchanges**: Peer-to-peer trading platforms facilitate the exchange of water allocations among users. These exchanges create a more dynamic, responsive and liquid water market, allowing for efficient reallocation of resources based on need and value.
4. **Smart Contracts**: Automated agreements enforce rules and regulations, ensuring compliance and reducing administrative overhead.
5. **Tokenization**: Water rights, entitlements and allocations are represented as digital tokens, enabling easy accounting, tracking, transfer, and trading.

2.2 Platform Architecture

The Water Ledger platform is built on a layered architecture:

1. **Blockchain Layer**: Utilizes Hedera blockchain for its robust smart contract capabilities, tokenization and consensus services, and commercialisation.

2. **Smart Contract Layer**: Implements the business logic, including the ERC3525 token standard for water rights management.
3. **API Layer**: Provides interfaces for integration with external systems and applications.
4. **User Interface Layer**: Offers intuitive web and mobile interfaces for users to interact with the platform.

2.3 Benefits of Water Ledger

The implementation of Water Ledger offers numerous benefits:

1. **Enhanced Transparency**: All transactions and water usage data are recorded on an immutable ledger, accessible to all stakeholders.
2. **Improved Efficiency**: Automated processes reduce administrative and compliance costs and enable faster, more secure transactions.
3. **Increased Trust**: The decentralized nature of blockchain eliminates the need for intermediaries and reduces the potential for fraud or manipulation.
4. **Better Resource Allocation**: Real-time data and efficient trading mechanisms allow for more responsive and optimal allocation of water.
5. **Regulatory Compliance**: Built-in rules and restrictions ensure adherence to regulatory requirements and sustainable water use practices.

3 Blockchain Technology in Water Ledger

Water Ledger leverages third-generation distributed ledger technology to create a secure, transparent, and efficient platform for water resource management.

3.1 Hedera Hashgraph

Water Ledger is built on the Hedera Hashgraph [3], chosen for its high performance, robust security, and low transaction costs making Water Ledger feasible for commercialisation. Hedera's unique hashgraph consensus algorithm provides near-instant finality and can handle hundreds of thousands of transactions per second, making it an ideal foundation for Water Ledger's sophisticated water accounting, management, and trading system.

Key advantages of Hedera for Water Ledger include:

1. **High Throughput**: Capable of processing over 10,000 transactions per second, ensuring Water Ledger can scale to meet the demands of global water accounting, management and trading systems.
2. **Low Latency**: Transactions achieve consensus in 3–5 s, enabling near real-time updates of water rights and trades.
3. **Fair Ordering**: Hedera's consensus algorithm ensures fair ordering of transactions, critical for a transparent water market.
4. **Low Fees**: Transaction fees on Hedera are a fraction of a cent, making it economically viable for frequent, small-scale water trades.
5. **Sustainability**: Hedera's proof-of-stake model is significantly more energy-efficient than traditional blockchain networks.

Water Ledger integrates with Hedera's native services where beneficial:

1. **Hedera Consensus Service (HCS)**: Used for ordering and timestamping of transactions, ensuring a verifiable record of all water rights operations.
2. **Hedera Token Service (HTS)**: While our core water rights are represented by our custom tokens, we utilize HTS for ancillary functions and to represent other types of assets within the Water Ledger ecosystem.

This allows Water Ledger to leverage the best of both worlds - the high performance and low cost of Hedera's native services, combined with the flexibility and customization of our own implementations.

3.2 Smart Contracts and Custom Implementation

While Hedera provides native services like the Hedera Consensus Service (HCS) and Hedera Token Service (HTS), Water Ledger goes beyond these offerings to create a more flexible and customized solution. We have developed our own smart contracts, implemented in Solidity, which can be deployed on Hedera's smart contract service.

Key components of our custom implementation include:

1. **Management Contract**: Handles the creation and management of water resources, classes, and products.
2. **Custom Token Contract**: Implements our ERC3525-inspired semi-fungible token standard for water rights.
3. **Exchange Contract**: Facilitates peer-to-peer trading of water allocations, entitlements and titles (water rights).

3.3 Custom ERC3525-Inspired Semi-Fungible Token Implementation

A cornerstone of Water Ledger's innovation is our custom implementation of an ERC3525-inspired [4] semi-fungible token standard. This implementation offers several key advantages:

1. **Portability**: By implementing our token standard in Solidity, we ensure that it can be easily ported to other blockchain platforms that support Solidity, reducing dependency on Hedera alone.
2. **Customization**: Our implementation is specifically tailored to the unique requirements of water rights accounting and management, offering functionalities that generic token standards may not provide.
3. **Flexibility**: The semi-fungible nature of our tokens allows for representation of both the unique aspects of water rights (such as location or type) and the fungible aspects (such as volume).
4. **Efficiency**: Our implementation optimizes for the specific use case of water rights, potentially offering gas savings and improved performance compared to more generic implementations.

3.4 Advantages of Custom Implementation

Our custom token implementation offers several benefits specific to Water Ledger:

1. **Water-Specific Attributes**: We can include attributes crucial for water rights accounting, management and trading, such as location, expiry dates, and water source, directly in the token structure.
2. **Complex Operations**: Our implementation supports complex operations specific to water rights, such as splitting water entitlements or merging rights, which may not be possible with standard token implementations.
3. **Regulatory Compliance**: We can embed regulatory requirements directly into the token logic, ensuring all transfers and trades comply with local water management rules.
4. **Improved Traceability**: Our custom implementation allows for detailed tracking of water rights history, including ownership, use, transfers, splits, and merges.
5. **Interoperability**: While optimized for Hedera, our Solidity-based implementation ensures interoperability with other blockchain platforms, future-proofing the Water Ledger system.

4 Conclusion and Future Outlook

Water Ledger represents a significant advancement in the application of blockchain technology to water resource management. By leveraging the innovative ERC3525 token standard and creating a user-centric platform, Water Ledger addresses many of the challenges facing traditional water management systems [5].

4.1 Key Contributions

1. **Enhanced Transparency**: Water Ledger provides a single source of truth for water rights and usage, increasing trust among stakeholders.
2. **Improved Efficiency**: Automated processes and peer-to-peer trading reduce administrative overhead and enable faster resource allocation.
3. **User Empowerment**: Individual water wallets give users greater control and visibility over their water rights.
4. **Technical Innovation**: The implementation of ERC3525 tokens offers a more flexible and efficient way to represent and manage water rights.
5. **Real-World Application**: The Seqwater implementation project demonstrates the practical benefits of blockchain in water management.

4.2 Challenges and Limitations

Despite its potential, Water Ledger faces several challenges:

1. **Regulatory Adaptation**: Widespread adoption will require changes to existing water management regulations.
2. **User Adoption**: Success depends on water users embracing new technology and changing established practices.
3. **Data Integration**: Integrating blockchain with existing water management systems and ensuring data accuracy remains complex.

4.3 Future Research Directions

Future work on Water Ledger should focus on:

1. Enhancing interoperability with other blockchain networks and traditional water management systems.
2. Exploring the application of AI and machine learning to improve water allocation and market price/volatility predictions and optimize trading strategies.
3. Investigating the potential of Water Ledger principles in managing other natural resources, such as carbon credits, water quality credits or critical mineral water stewardship mandates.

In conclusion, Water Ledger demonstrates the transformative potential of blockchain technology in addressing one of the world's most pressing challenges – sustainable water resource management. As water scarcity continues to be a global concern, innovative solutions like Water Ledger will play a crucial role in ensuring equitable and efficient water use for future generations.

References

1. UN Water. The United Nations World Water Development Report 2021: Valuing Water. UNESCO, Paris (2021)
2. Water Ledger Australia. Water Ledger: Transforming Water Management with Blockchain Technology. White Paper (2021)
3. Hedera Hashgraph, LLC. Hedera: A Public Distributed Ledger and Governing Council. Technical Whitepaper (2022)
4. Ethereum Foundation. EIP-3525: Semi-Fungible Token. Ethereum Improvement Proposals (2022)
5. World Economic Forum. Building Block(chain)s for a Better Planet. Fourth Industrial Revolution for the Earth Series (2018)

Digital Identity Wallet Utilizing a Hardware Security Module

Paul Ashley[1](✉), Gowri Ramachandran[2], Ellen Schofield[2], and George Mulhearn[1]

[1] Anonyome Labs, Gold Coast, Qld 4217, Australia
{pashley,gmulhearn}@anonyome.com
[2] Queensland University of Technology, Brisbane, Qld 4000, Australia
g.ramachandran@qut.edu.au, ellen.schofield@connect.qut.edu.au

Abstract. New European standards for the EU Digital Identity Wallet mandates support for a Hardware Security Module (HSM). This module is able to perform important cryptographic operations providing very strong security and privacy protection for a user. The EU Digital Identity Wallet is typically an application the user installs on an iOS or Android mobile device allowing the user to manage their government and commercial issued verifiable credentials. Fulfilling the requirements of the EU Digital Identity Wallet, this paper outlines how an existing Digital Identity Wallet can be enhanced to leverage a HSM, examining both inbuilt and external implementations. This paper presents a compatible matrix by analyzing the existing credential standards and different HSM cryptographic capabilities.

Keywords: eIDAS · EU DI Wallet · Decentralized Identity · Verifiable Credentials · Hardware Security Module

1 Introduction

Decentralized Identity is a new paradigm in identity and access management [1]. Instead of the user using a centralized process (creating an account on a service) or a federated process (social login from an identity provider), a user has a Digital Identity Wallet that holds their decentralized identifiers, cryptographic keys, and verifiable credentials. The wallet is used to connect to a service, and to present and receive verifiable credentials. The main motivation for this new paradigm is to provide greater security and privacy for users when interacting online.

The most common form factor for a Digital Identity Wallet is an application on a mobile device. Installed from the AppStore or PlayStore this Digital Identity Wallet is designed to allow a user to participate fully in one or more decentralized identity based ecosystems e.g. finance, travel, education, health care.

Verifiable credentials [2] are signed, tamper-proof documents issued to a Holder (user) into their Digital Identity Wallet. The verifiable credential may contain the user's decentralized identifier, binding the credential to the user. When requested to present their credentials to a verifier (also called a relying party) the Digital Identity Wallet responds with a verifiable presentation, signed by the bound Holder (user), which embeds the

S. Kanhere et al. (Eds.): SDLT 2024, CCIS 2453, pp. 125–136, 2025.
https://doi.org/10.1007/978-981-96-4442-1_9

verifiable credential/s, signed by the Issuer. This process ensures the verifier can trust the data contained in the verifiable credential and verify that the Digital Identity Wallet is the intended Holder.

So that a user's decentralized identifier and verifiable credentials cannot be misused (e.g. stolen into another user's wallet) it is advisable to use Hardware Security Modules (HSMs). These security modules provide cryptographic operations: creating private/public key pairs, exporting public keys, decrypting/signing of data. An important concept in HSM-based wallets is maintaining a high level of assurance. Multiple previous studies have examined this concept through mobile identity wallets and identified common challenges [3–5]. First, the challenge of key binding where cryptographic keys are bound to verifiable credentials which are bound to user wallets. [5, 6] considers the approach of key binding through a Secure Enclave, StrongBox Keymaster, KeyAttestation, BiometricPrompt and SafetyNet API to develop a secure solution. The Secure Enclave is specific to iOS devices whilst the others are native to Android. The design generates a cryptographic key pair inside trusted hardware, on the user's smartphone, through these native tools and APIs.

This paper focuses on the steps to add HSM support to an existing Digital Identity Wallet. The paper describes two different form factors. First using the built in secure enclave that is available in modern mobile devices, and second to use an external hardware device. The motivation behind this work is alignment with the new EU regulations around Digital Identity Wallets.

2 EU Digital Identity Wallet Hardware Security Module Requirements

The European Commission has adopted a recommendation calling on member states to work towards the development of a technical Architecture and Reference Framework (ARF) [7], a set of common standards and technical specifications and a set of common guidelines and best practices for a Digital Identity Framework.

The Commission intends to use this ARF to develop the EU DI Wallet reference implementation. The EU DI Wallet is primarily designed to facilitate a number of use cases through the implementation of decentralized identity verifiable credentials:

- Identification and authentication to access online services
- Qualified electronic signature
- Mobile driving licence
- Pseudonyms
- Health
- Educational credentials and professional qualifications
- Digital finance
- Digital travel credential

The EU DI Wallet providers are commercial software companies delivering implementations for the member states. It is expected that each member state of the EU will provide to its citizens a compliant EU DI Wallet.

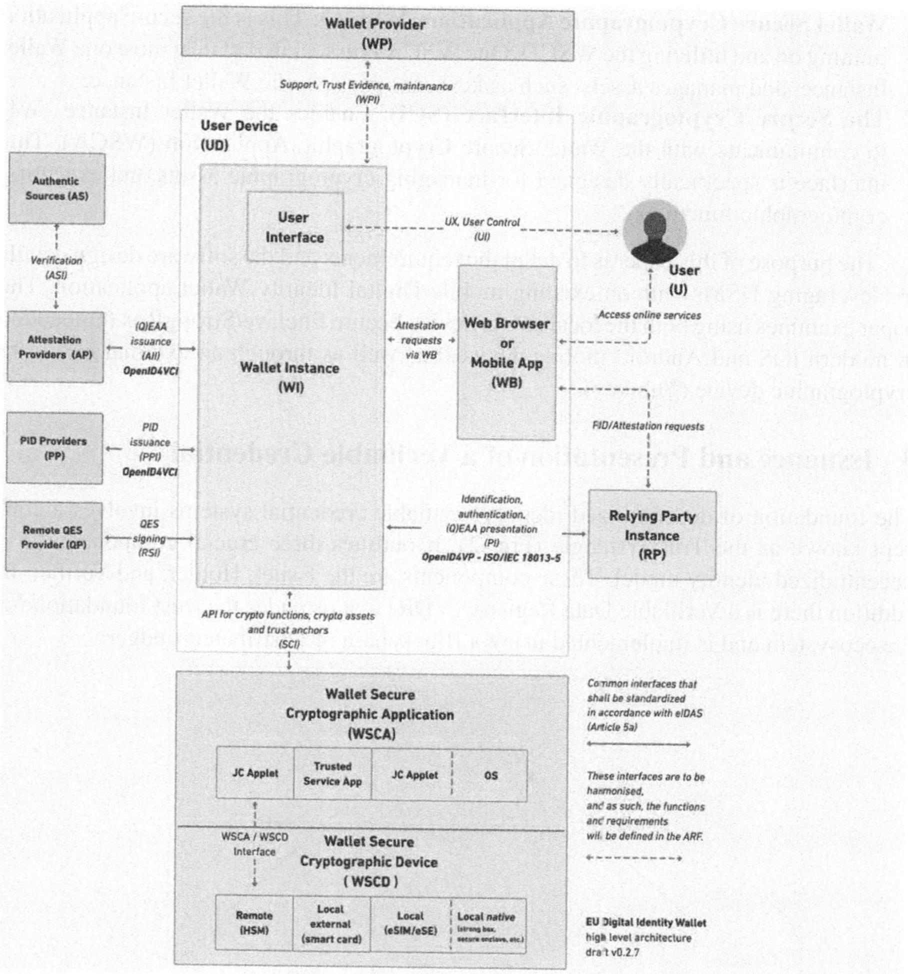

Fig. 1. Architecture of the EU DI Wallet ecosystem and its components

Figure 1 shows an overview of the architecture of the EUDI Wallet ecosystem and its components as outlined in the ARF. **The Wallet Instance (WI),** which is usually a mobile application for iOS and Android, will utilize specialized cryptographic hardware (text taken directly from the ARF):

- **Wallet Secure Cryptographic Device (WSCD):** This is trusted hardware providing a secure environment and storage for cryptographic assets (such as keys) and for running the WSCA. This includes the keystore but also the environment where the security-critical functions are executed. The WSCD is tamper-proof and duplication-proof. One WSCD may be used by multiple Wallet Instances, e.g. in case of a HSM. The WSCD consists of two parts: the WSCD hardware covers the hardware issued by the WSCD vendor and the WSCD firmware covers security-related software, such as operating system and cryptographic libraries provided by the WSCD vendor.

- **Wallet Secure Cryptographic Application (WSCA):** This is the secure application running on and utilizing the WSCD. One WSCA is associated with at most one Wallet Instance, and manages assets, such as keys, for this specific Wallet Instance.
- **The Secure Cryptographic Interface (SCI)**: Enables the Wallet Instance (WI) to communicate with the Wallet Secure Cryptographic Application (WSCA). This interface is specifically designed for managing cryptographic assets and executing cryptographic functions.

The purpose of this paper is to detail the requirements and the software design details for leveraging HSMs with an existing mobile Digital Identity Wallet application. The paper examines using both the local native device Secure Enclave/StrongBox (embedded in modern iOS and Android mobile devices) as well as through an external hardware cryptographic device (Yubikey).

3 Issuance and Presentation of a Verifiable Credential

The foundation of decentralized identity verifiable credential systems involves a concept known as the Trust Triangle (Fig. 2). It outlines three crucial components in a decentralized identity model. These components are the Issuer, Holder, and Verifier. In addition there is a Verifiable Data Registry (VDR) that provides the trust foundation for the ecosystem and is implemented using a Blockchain or Distributed Ledger.

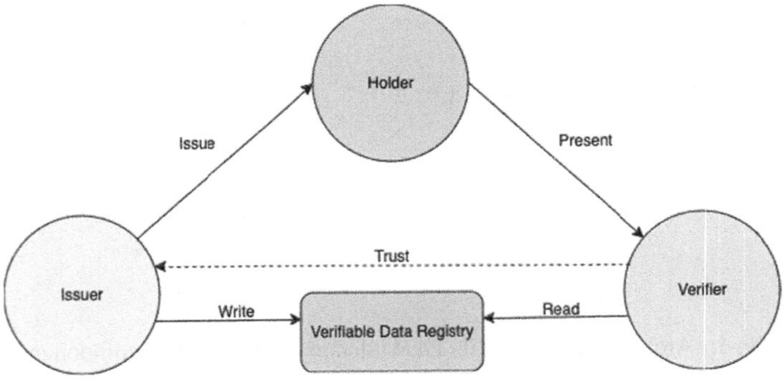

Fig. 2. Verifiable Credentials "Trust Triangle"

The Issuer is responsible for issuing verifiable credentials which contain Personally Identifiable Information (PII) about a Holder. The Issuer must have their Decentralized Identifier (DID) registered with a VDR where it is classified as a trusted authority. Passports, driver licenses, education qualifications, and numerous other examples can be implemented as verifiable credentials.

During creation, these credentials are signed by the Issuer's private key. Additionally, the Issuer DID and Holder DID are bound to the issued credential. Once the Holder receives the credential it is stored in the Holder's Digital Identity Wallet.

The Holder can then present their verifiable credentials to a Verifier where the claims can be verified as legitimate. The Verifier receives a presentation proof from the Holder which contains the digital signatures from the Issuer and the Holder.

The Verifier reads from the Verifiable Data Registry to find the associated Issuer public key and DID.

There is no point in this process where the Verifier and Issuer should communicate with each other. Through cryptographic proofs the Verifier can trust that the Holder credential originated from the Issuer, know that it is bound to the Holder, that it hasn't been tampered with, and that it hasn't been revoked.

The sequence diagram outlined in Fig. 3 displays a more detailed view of the sequence of operations involved with issuing and presenting a credential. It focuses on use of the Hardware Security Module for supporting the verifiable credential signatures.

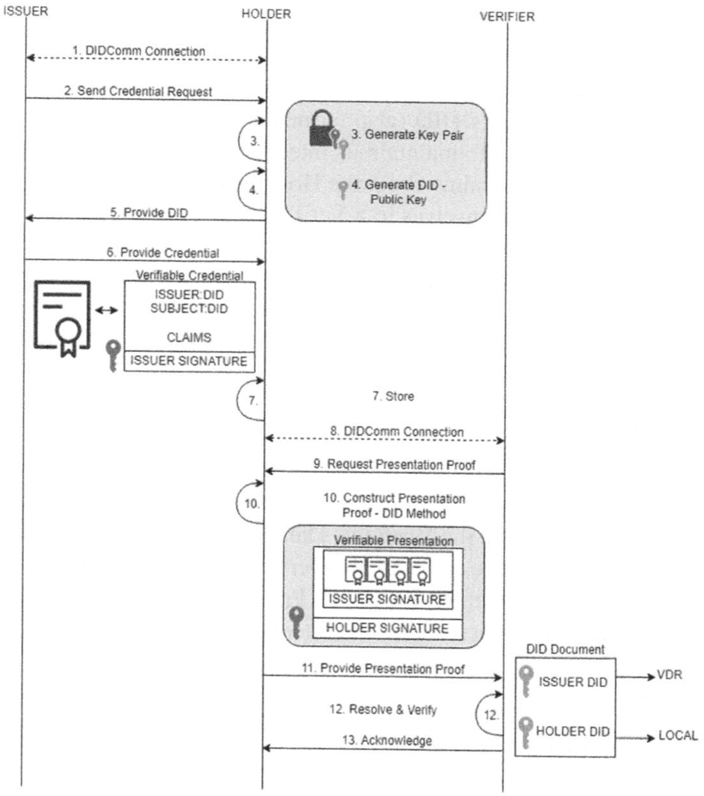

Fig. 3. Detailed Issuing and Presentation of a Verifiable Credential

The first operation (1) is the initialization of a secure connection through DIDComm. This enables the Issuer and Holder to communicate with each other knowing that the communications are end-to-end encrypted (E2EE) and both parties are sure the information sent/received is to/from the correct party.

Once the connection has been established, the Issuer sends the Holder a credential offer (2). If the Holder doesn't have a cryptographic key pair already, it will be generated. This operation is the first example where the trusted cryptographic hardware is used:

- *The cryptographic private/public key pair is generated within a Hardware Security Module (3). Depending on the implementation choice it is either in the Secure Enclave/StrongBox in the mobile phone itself or using an external Hardware Security Module.*
- *The generated private key never leaves the Hardware Security Module. This maintains complete integrity of the private key and ensures that it cannot be tampered with or stolen.*
- *The public key is exported from the Hardware Security Module and used within the Digital Identity Wallet to create a unique identifier known as a Holder DID (4).*

Depending on the DID Method, the Holder's DID can also be uploaded to the Verifiable Data Registry.

Once the Holder's DID has been created and provided to the Issuer (5), the Issuer is then able to create a verifiable credential and send to the Holder (6). This verifiable credential includes the Holder's DID (also termed a Subject DID) and is signed with the private key from the Issuer to maintain its integrity and provide proof of origin. The verifiable credential contains claims about the Holder of which the Holder can use later to prove information about themselves to a Verifier. The Holder can store the obtained verifiable credential in their Digital Identity Wallet (7).

Later the Holder can establish a DIDComm connection (8) with the Verifier so that a Verifier can request a Presentation Proof (9). The construction of the Presentation Proof utilizes the Holder's DID key, and is the next place where the Hardware Security Module is used:

- *Once the Presentation Proof is created, the Holder signs the Proof with their private key within the Hardware Security Module (10).*

The Presentation Proof is then given to the Verifier (11) to check the validity of the credential. The Verifier will use the Verifiable Data Registry to return the Issuer's public key to verify the Issuer signature, and will also verify the Holder's signature (again using the Holder's public key). Once the Presentation Proof has been verified (12), the Holder is sent an acknowledgement that the Verifier either approves or disapproves the provided credential (13).

4 Hardware Security Modules

This project experimented with two types of Hardware Security Modules. The first type is built into modern mobile devices, the iOS Secure Enclave [8, 9] and Android StrongBox [10]. The second is an external device, a Yubikey [11].

4.1 iOS Secure Enclave

The iOS Secure Enclave is different in terms of implementation but shares the same purpose as the Android StrongBox. That is, to protect private keys through software and hardware isolation. It's a dedicated secure subsystem which is integrated into Apple SoCs

[8]. The Secure Enclave also features its own Apple-customised version of the L4 microkernel which is SepOS [8]. This processor is only dedicated for Secure Enclave functionality which minimizes the chances of side-channel attacks. The use of Apple's Keychain API enables interfacing with the Secure Enclave to generate protected cryptographic keys.

4.2 Android StrongBox

StrongBox is a feature which leverages a software and hardware isolated environment provided by the Secure Element. Much like the iOS Secure Enclave, generated private keys are never exposed outside the hardware. This ensures complete protection and integrity of the private key. Even if the device is compromised, StrongBox remains protected due to its isolation. The same outcomes can be achieved through a Trusted Execution Environment (TEE), although StrongBox has better security guarantees against physical and side-channel attacks [10]. The key difference is that a TEE is an isolated environment on the main processor, whereas Android StrongBox is completely separate. Interfacing with Android StrongBox or the Trusted Execution Environment is done through the Android Keystore API.

4.3 Yubikey

Yubikeys [11] are a range of dedicated hardware authentication devices which support numerous modern and legacy authentication protocols, including WebAuthn/FIDO, OpenPGP and smart card authentication. The Yubikey 5C device (Fig. 4) used in this paper differs from StrongBox and Secure Enclave in that it's a portable solution; taking the form of a small USB-sized device that communicate with mobile devices and computers via NFC or USB. This allows users to use their Yubikey authenticator with multiple different devices, so long as they physically hold the key.

Fig. 4. Yuibkey 5C Device

5 Compatible Cryptographies

One of the areas that needed investigation early was the cryptographic compatibility for the Hardware Security Modules. The compatibility of iOS Secure Enclave, Android StrongBox and Yubikey hardware to meet the decentralized identity verifiable credentials standards is shown in Table 1.

Table 1 contains four different credential standards – Hyperledger AnonCreds [12], W3C credentials [2], IETF SD-JWT [14] and ISO-18013-5 [13] (also called the mobile driver's license or MDL). The table lists the most common cryptography used with each. The right four columns show the cryptographic support in iOS, Android and Yubikey (via OpenPGP or WebAuthn signing modes). As can be seen the cryptographic capabilities of the Hardware Security Modules in the mobile devices is more limited than for Yubikey which has broader cryptographic support.

Table 1. Compatibility Matrix for Hardware Security Module Cryptography

Standard	Verifiable Presentation Format	Cryptography	Android	iOS	Yubikey OpenPGP	WebAuthn Authenticators (Yubikey, etc)
W3C VCDM	JSON-LD Data Integrity Proof	P-256	✓	✓	✓	✓*
		RSA	✓	✗	✓	✗
		Ed25519	✗	✗	✓	✓*
		BBS+	✗	✗	✗	✗
	JWT	P-256	✓	✓	✓	✓*
		RSA	✓	✗	✓	✗
		Ed25519	✗	✗	✓	✓*
IETF SD-JWT	SD-JWT	P-256	✓	✓	✓	✓*
		RSA	✓	✗	✓	✗
		Ed25519	✗	✗	✓	✓*
Hyperledger AnonCreds	Anoncreds V1	CL AnonCreds (ZKP)	✗	✗	✗	✗
ISO 18013-5	ISO mDL	P-256	✓	✓	✓	✗
		Ed25519	✗	✗	✓	✗

* WebAuthn authenticator signatures for P256 & Ed25519 are not *raw* signatures over arbitrary data, they are signatures over the arbitrary data + some WebAuthn headers. As such, they can be seen as *variants* of P256 & Ed25519 signatures as the verifier needs to understand the WebAuthn context to verify the signature. This context can only be given in formats which support custom cryptography suites to be defined.

6 Software Implementation

The starting point of this project was a Digital Identity Wallet constructed using an underlying Wallet SDK (also known as the Edge Agent SDK). The Edge Agent SDK provides an implementation of credential exchange protocols (Aries/DIDComm, ...), credential implementation (AnonCreds, W3C credentials, ...) and a wallet storage. The wallet storage is provided by an open-source library called Aries Askar that also provides the cryptographic implementation. It works as follows (Fig. 5):

- the underlying Edge Agent SDK (Rust library) can create keys and sign data using software enclave (based on the Aries Askar Rust library)
- the Edge Agent SDK (Rust library) is exported via UniFFI (Foreign Function Interface (FFI) wrapper) to be used by the iOS and Android Edge Agent SDK (native SDKs, Kotlin & Swift)
- the Native Wallet apps (iOS & Android) consume the Edge Agent SDK (native SDKs, Kotlin & Swift) implementation

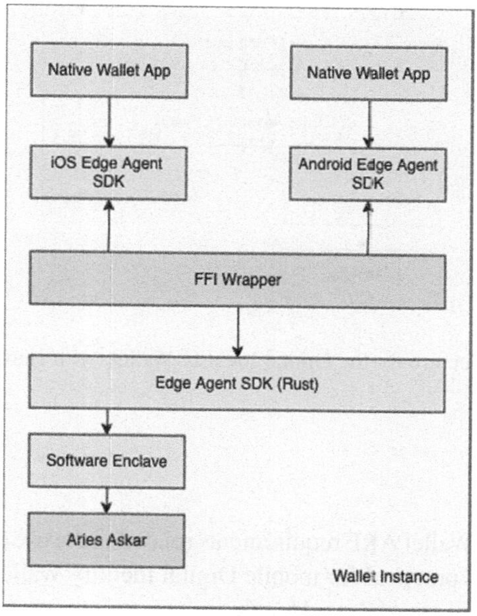

Fig. 5. Software Architecture for the Digital Identity Wallet (no Hardware Security Module)

The Digital Identity Wallet was then enhanced to use the Hardware Security Module by supplementing the Edge Agent SDK leveraging both the local and external Hardware Security Modules. It works as follows (Fig. 6):

- the EdgeAgent SDK (Rust) can create keys and sign data by interfacing with a new abstract *Wallet Secure Cryptographic Device (WSCD)*
- the EdgeAgent SDK (Rust) is exported via UniFFI (FFI wrapper) to be used by the iOS and Android Edge Agent SDK (native SDKs, Kotlin & Swift)
- the iOS and Android Edge Agent SDKs define it's own WSCD implementation, which is passed/plugged into the Edge Agent SDK (Rust) via UniFFI (so that Rust can call onto it)

- the iOS and Android Edge Agent SDK's WSCD is designed to support a number of different WSCDs. Including local WSCDs (Secure Enclave, StrongBox), external WSCDs (YubiKey), and potentially others in the future
- the Native Wallet apps (iOS & Android) consume the Edge Agent SDK

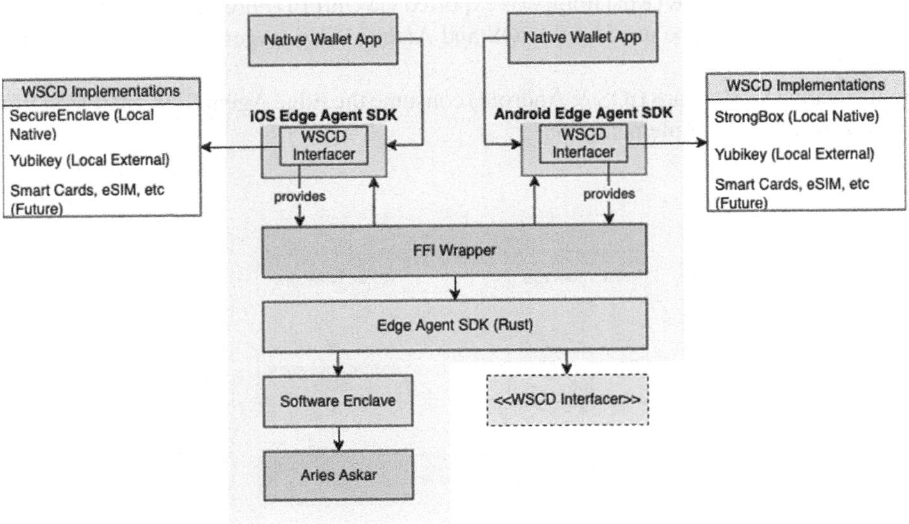

Fig. 6. Software Architecture for the Digital Identity Wallet (with Hardware Security Module)

7 Conclusions

Supporting the EU DI Wallet ARF requirements related to the use of a Hardware Security Module is feasible and practical for mobile Digital Identity Wallet applications. But the implementer must be aware of the tradeoffs.

7.1 Algorithmic Compatibility

Hardware Security Modules offer the best protection for private key storage and cryptographic operations as they are isolated, tamper and side channel attack resistant.

There are cryptographic limitations when using the native iOS Secure Enclave and Android StrongBox. These implementations provide more limited cryptographic support and therefore are currently not suitable for the full range of credential types currently being used. Using an external Yubikey device has been found to be more algorithmically flexible.

An embedded alternative to using the iOS Secure Enclave or Android Strongbox is the use of eSIM/eUICC or eSE. Both are recognized as options in the ARF documentation. The adoption of these technologies can improve algorithmic interoperability in the embedded solutions by allowing over the network software updates instead of a user having to replace to newer mobile hardware.

7.2 User Experience

An advantage of the use of an embedded Hardware Security Module in the mobile device (via the Secure Enclave/StrongBox) is the convenience and reliability. The user only needs their mobile phone and can interact securely using their Hardware Security Module without needing a separate device.

However, in this embedded configuration, the user wallet is restricted to a single device without an option to backup or share as it's device bound.

The external Hardware Security Module implemented with the Yubikey device provides portability for the user. The Yubikey device can be used across multiple of the user's mobile devices meaning mobile device replacement or using multiple devices is easier for the user.

The drawback of external HSMs, like Yubikey, is the requirement to physically carry and interact with the external device to perform cryptographic operations. Whenever the Digital Identity Wallet user wishes to create a DID or present credentials, they are required to physically plug in their device, or connect to it wirelessly (e.g., NFC).

7.3 Performance

The cryptographic performance of the HSM is not a major concern due to the low frequency that HSM operations (create keypair and sign data) are expected to occur for a Digital Identity Wallet end-user. Although HSMs are anticipated to perform slower than on-device cryptography, overhead in the milliseconds are unlikely to impact the overall user experience in comparison to other factors. This is particularly the case in external HSMs, where the significant time bottleneck will come from the relatively slow user experience of having to physically interact with the device.

References

1. Innovating Identity and Access Management with Decentralized Identity. https://sudoplatform.com/2022/10/innovating-identity-and-access-management-with-decentralized-identity/. Accessed 15 July 2024
2. Verifiable Credentials Data Model v2.0. https://www.w3.org/TR/vc-data-model-2.0/. Accessed 15 July 2024
3. Larsen, B., Kassem, N.E., Chen, L.: Achieving higher level of assurance in privacy preserving identity wallets. In: International Conference on Trust, Security and Privacy in Computing and Communications (2023)
4. Czerny, R., Kollmann, C., Podgorelec, B., Prunster, B., Zefferer, T.: Smoothing the ride: providing a seamless upgrade path from established cross-border eID workflows towards eID wallet systems. In: SECRYPT 2023 - Proceedings of the 20th International Conference on Security and Cryptography (2023)
5. Spychalski, D., Rode, O., Ritthaler, M., Raptis, G.: Conceptual design and analysis of a mobile digital identity for eHealth applications. In: 2021 IEEE EMBS International Conference on Biomedical and Health Informatics (BHI) (2021)
6. Mayrhofer, R., Stoep, J.V., Brubaker, C., Kralevich, N.: The android platform security model. In: 2023 ACM Transactions on Privacy and Security (2023)

7. European Digital Identity Wallet Architecture and Reference Framework.https://github.com/eu-digital-identity-wallet/eudi-doc-architecture-and-reference-framework/blob/main/docs/arf.md. Accessed 12 July 2024
8. Secure Enclave iOS Documentation. https://developer.apple.com/documentation/security/certificate_key_and_trust_services/keys/protecting_keys_with_the_secure_enclave. Accessed 12 July 2024
9. Secure Enclave iOS Design, https://support.apple.com/en-au/guide/security/sec59b0b31X/web
10. Android KeyStore System. https://developer.android.com/privacy-and-security/keystore
11. Yubico Support Matrix. https://support.yubico.com/hc/en-us/articles/360016649139-YubiKey-5-2-Enhancements-to-OpenPGP-3-4-Support
12. AnonCreds Specification v1.0 Draft. https://hyperledger.github.io/anoncredsspec/. Accessed 15 July 2024
13. ISO/IEC 18013–5:2021 Personal identification—ISO-compliant driving licencePart 5: Mobile driving licence (mDL) application. https://www.iso.org/standard/69084.html
14. Selective Disclosure for JWTs (SD-JWT) draft-ietf-oauth-selective-disclosure-jwt-12. https://datatracker.ietf.org/doc/draft-ietf-oauth-selective-disclosure-jwt/

Author Index

S. Kanhere et al. (Eds.): SDLT 2024, CCIS 2453, p. 137, 2025.
https://doi.org/10.1007/978-981-96-4442-1